KIDS AND
CORNBREAD CAKES

Based on the True Story of One "Incredible" Life

Alisah Horne

ISBN: 1530193567
ISBN 13: 9781530193561
Library of Congress Control Number: 2016903331
CreateSpace Independent Publishing Platform
North Charleston, South Carolina

DISCLAIMER

This story is based on actual persons, events, and locales from information gathered through interviews, memories, and conversations. In some instances, in order to fully express the personalities of the characters, I have interjected my own thoughts. In order to maintain anonymity and protect the privacy of individuals, some of the names, identifying characteristics, locales, and details have been changed.

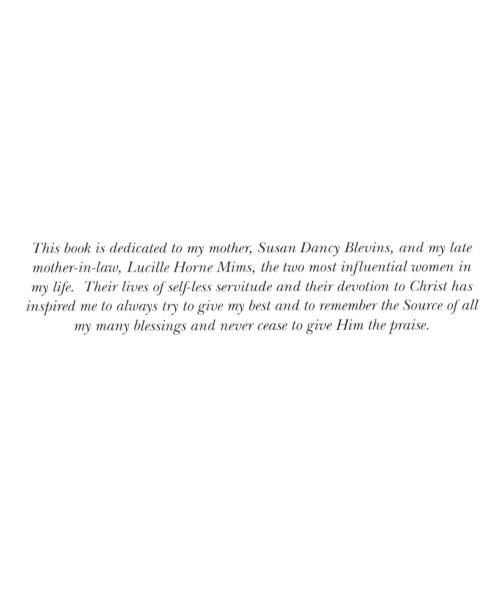

This book is dedicated to my mother, Susan Dancy Blevins, and my late mother-in-law, Lucille Horne Mims, the two most influential women in my life. Their lives of self-less servitude and their devotion to Christ has inspired me to always try to give my best and to remember the Source of all my many blessings and never cease to give Him the praise.

ACKNOWLEDGEMENTS

I would like to say a special thank you to my husband, Ronnie Horne, who was my strength, to Barbara Horne Rosser, Robert Horne, and Bernice Blackburn for sharing their memories, and to my mother, Susan Blevins, who was my sounding board and my greatest fan.

I would also like to thank my friend, Laura Welborn, for believing in me and encouraging me throughout the process of writing this book.

Finally, I would like to thank Eunice Call, my writing mentor and faithful friend. Your wonderful writings and stories have so inspired me to write down on paper all the stories I love to tell.

ABOUT THE AUTHOR

Alisah Horne is a lifelong resident of North Carolina, having grown up in the foothills of the Blue Ridge Mountains. She resides with Ronnie Horne, her husband and the love of her life. Alisah's deeply rooted love of story sharing began in infancy on her "Granddaddy Minter's" knee. She listened with rapt attention when Lucy, the subject of this book, shared her life story over the years. Through years of working with children and acquiring certification in literacy programs like Motheread®, Inc, Raising a Reader, and Read to Me, she experienced firsthand the positive impact that reading to children and placing books into their hands can have. Through funds raised from her storytelling business, *Tales Worth Telling*, Alisah continues to provide stories and books to children throughout Wilkes County.

PROLOGUE

I step outside into the crisp night air. It is a moonless night, but the sky is alight in a warm glow. There are at least a million more stars out tonight than ever before. I imagine that God is walking across the sky lighting all the stars, even those dimmed by time. He is lighting all those extra stars to make sure Lucy does not miss that narrow path. I smile at the thought.

I know Lucy has already found that narrow path and reached the pearly gate. As a child I learned that heaven's gate was constructed of a single pearl, and I pictured a monster size oyster creating that pearl.

I can picture Lucy's arrival at that gate. It is not a gate in the sense we envision, but it is a gate into the past, present, and future. It is a place of eternal rest, where Lucy can spend the next ninety-three years, recounting her life, and that will only be the beginning.

I imagine Lucy taking in a deep breath, and in the presence of perfect peace saying, "There is no better place to start than the beginning."

As her eyes fade back in time, she swallows hard, and it is as if those ninety-three years just melt away, and she is back to her beginning.

CHAPTER ONE

A whole lifetime ago Saltville, Virginia was my starting point. It was a hot, stagnant, muggy July day in our southern Virginia mountain town. My daddy, Moe Elmore, was working in the salt mine, and my momma, Ester, already one week overdue, was trying to tend to my older brother, Will.

Around suppertime, Momma began having pains, and Daddy sent for the midwife. Momma laid there ringing her hands and praying for a daughter. Since childhood, she had been plagued with premonitions and dreams of dying young, and these dreams had continued into her teenage years. She knew in her heart that she would not live into old age, and she so wanted a daughter- me- so I could help care for the family in case these premonitions proved true. Momma picked out my name long before my birth. She named me Lucy which means bringer of light. She said that when she saw me she knew I would be a bright light to everyone I came into contact.

Momma later gave birth to my two sisters Bonnie and Bessie, but of us four she said I was the easiest- labor and delivery lasting a mere three hours from start to finish. Momma said that I arrived in a halo of soft blonde hair and the brightest blue eyes that even at birth showed a soul that was full of love. I really like to think that was true.

Momma said she immediately fell in love with me and spent the rest of the evening counting my fingers and toes and singing the new song she made up just for me - the song she would sing to me until the day she died.

My baby Lucy, with hair of blonde and eyes of blue
I know you will grow up to be honest and true
Where ever life takes you, be it close or far away
I will love my little Lucy till my dying day.

As July 23rd 1920, my birth day, came to a close Momma whispered to Daddy, "Everything will get better now," and she drifted off into a sweet sleep with me snuggled on her chest.

CHAPTER TWO

We moved to Wilkesboro, North Carolina, a little town nestled in the foothills of the Blue Ridge Mountains, when I was a year old so Daddy could work in the cotton mill.

Momma wasted no time in training me, as I was only eighteen months old when Bonnie was born. Bonnie was a fussy baby and cried most of her waking hours, taking all of Momma's time and energy. I never remember being jealous; after all, I was the big sister and Momma needed my help now more than ever. Will, my big brother, helped to look after me and I, in turn, helped Momma look after Bonnie.

I was almost four when my baby sister, Bessie, was born. I fell in love with her at first sight. She had the curliest blonde hair and the rosiest red cheeks, and I knew she was the prettiest baby ever born. Momma would let me hold her on my lap, and I would pretend that she was my baby.

Bonnie was not happy that Bessie had taken her position in the family. Bonnie continued to require most of Momma's time, as she was very stubborn, with the Moe Elmore temper, as Momma called it.

Momma began to wear down after Bessie's birth, and I over-heard a conversation she had with Daddy one night after all of us kids were in bed. She told Daddy that she was having terrible nightmares of dying and she was afraid she did not have much time left. Daddy responded with, "Ester, only the Good Lord knows when He plans to call you home, and you need to stop all this nonsense and get back to tending to these four kids the Good Lord has given us."

Momma never talked about her premonitions again, but you could see in her eyes that death was on her mind, and she needed to pack a whole lot of living and training into what time she had left. In fact, Momma began teaching me to cook when I was just five years old. She would put cornmeal, milk, eggs, and oil in a bowl and let me stir it until it was the exact consistency needed for cornbread cakes. She would then pull a chair over to the stove. After warning me not to touch it, she would have me stand in the chair, and I would watch her fry that cornbread mixture into crisp cakes.

By the time I was eight years old, I was capable of cooking and tending to most of the household chores. I remember Momma telling Daddy that she had taught me well. I remember whispering to myself, I hope she will teach me everything she knows because I want to grow up to be just like her.

CHAPTER THREE

S pring arrived like a lion that March of 1929. The weather was brutally cold one day and unseasonably warm the next. Momma told me that it was just the kind of weather that makes you sick. In fact, Momma was not feeling well herself. She just shrugged it off as an offending spring cold. Within a few days Momma could not pull herself off the bed. She was burning with fever and having difficulty breathing, and I was really scared. Daddy also feared the worst and sent Will to get Dr. Bauguess. After a thorough examination, Dr. Bauguess determined Momma had the flu with a touch of bronchitis and prescribed an onion poultice for her chest, cough syrup made from whiskey and rock candy, and a few days of bed rest. Daddy, Will, and I took over tending to the family.

While Daddy worked at the cotton mill each day, Will and I stayed home from school to take care of Momma. With Bonnie and Bessie at school, Will and I tended to the chores, and I cooked for us. Momma tried to help, but she was so weak and short of breath that she could not journey far from her bed. I remember running out of onions for her chest poultice and searching the yard for wild onions to use. The little wild onions I did find did not seem to be as potent as the ones we had managed to keep over from last year's garden.

Two weeks passed, then a month, and Momma did not seem to be getting any better, and I was starting to really worry. I began to think that maybe all those premonitions and dreams Momma had were about to come true. Will and I returned to school, and Daddy hired an old maid we called Aunt Rouge to tend to Momma while Daddy was at work.

I would often sneak away and cry. I wanted my momma, and I needed her as much as she had needed me to be born. I remembered the story behind my name, and I knew I had to be a bright light, especially now. Momma's favorite saying, "*It's a great life if you don't weaken, but who wants to be strong,*" resounded in my mind over and over.

As I witnessed Momma getting weaker and weaker in the coming months, I just wanted to scream at her, "I hate that quote- You need to be strong so I can stay strong, and it is only a great life if you do stay strong!"

In later years, I would understand the real meaning behind that saying and would even recite it to my own children, but for now I just needed my momma so much.

CHAPTER FOUR

In October of the same year, the whole world seemed to be coming apart at the seams, but it would be early December before we heard rumblings about the Great Depression. Daddy and I went to Plumber's Store to get a sack of meal and more rock candy for Momma's cough syrup, and I overheard Mr. Plumber talking about the stock market crash. He said that the crash had caused many men to jump to their deaths. I thought, why would men kill themselves over their livestock dying?

As Daddy and I walked home from the store, I asked him why so many men killed themselves because their farm animals died. Daddy chuckled and then told me it had nothing to do with their livestock but their money. They killed themselves because they lost all their money, and they just could not cope with that loss. I knew they sure must have had a whole lot more money than me because I could not imagine killing myself if I lost the twenty-two cents in my piggy bank.

It would be some time before we felt the effects of the Great Depression, but in early December of 1931 that Great Depression hit home. Daddy was still working at the cotton mill, and we still had Aunt Rouge staying with Momma. Momma took a turn for the worse around the time the cotton mill began a big lay- off. Daddy took a voluntary lay-off so he could tend to Momma.

By February of 1932, all Daddy's paper money had been spent from the coffee can, and all that remained was the silver change. The Great Depression had gravely affected the banking industry, and many banks were failing. Even the small community bank in our little town was not loaning money to farmers and millworkers because of the uncertainty of repayment. Daddy said we needed to pray that the Good Lord would take care of us. The Good Lord did see us through, but we had tough times ahead.

Since Momma took sick, I had become the main cook in the house, and the food supply was getting scarce. For the remainder of the winter, we ate potatoes saved from last summer's crop and the occasional treat of one of the dozen cans of tomatoes from our summer garden. I would also roam the woods trying to find an egg to fry for Momma as she was getting weaker and weaker, and I knew she needed the protein. Momma had been sick for over two years now. I had gotten use to the constant coughing and heavy breathing, but I was not at all prepared for what lay on the horizon.

CHAPTER FIVE

M arch of 1932 arrived like a lamb. Winter seemed a distant past and the earth was waking up from her long, deep sleep. The flowers were already abloom and the robins had already arrived back from their long southern vacation. Everyone and everything seemed to be revitalized and energized- that is, everyone but Momma. I was so hoping that when the days warmed she too would get her newly found energy source and everything would get back to normal.

I remember going in to feed Momma one morning in early March. I cracked open the window so she could hear the birds singing their new spring songs. I noticed that Momma's breathing was more labored. I knew Momma could see the fear in my eyes because she pulled me tight to her chest and sang that song she had sung to me since the day I was born:

My baby Lucy with hair of blonde and eyes of blue
I know you will grow up to be honest and true

Where ever life takes you be it close or far away
I will love my little Lucy until my dying day.

After she finished singing, she took my face in her hands and pulled me up until we were looking eye to eye, and she said, "You are my bright light; never forget it. I wanted you before you were ever born and I need you to be strong."

Momma's quote raced through my mind, "*It's a great life if you don't weaken, but who wants to be strong.*"

I was well on my way to learning what these words meant because March of 1932 was going to go out like a lion.

CHAPTER SIX

Later on that same week, in the wee hours before daylight, I heard Momma scream out from one of her nightmares. Seconds later, I heard Daddy's voice soothing Momma and telling her everything was alright. I laid there in my bed still as a mouse, but I could see and hear my heart pounding from under the bed covers. The screaming woke Bessie as well, and she came to my room. I scooped her into my bed and stroked her fine, blonde hair until she was sound asleep. I was unable to find sleep for the remainder of the night. I could not get my momma out of my mind. I thought about how sweet and beautiful she had always been even through her long sickness. I thought about all those stories she told me about my birth and how much she wanted me, and I thought about her premonitions and dreams. Then I thought, did Momma scream out tonight because of one of those dying dreams? I tried to think happy thoughts about butterflies and babies, but I could not get Momma off my mind and the screaming and the nightmares.

Morning could not come soon enough. I got up early and cooked fried potatoes for breakfast, and when Daddy came into the kitchen I told him about all the dark thoughts I was having about Momma. Daddy looked me straight in the eye and said, "Lucy, if you have a bad thought get it out of your mind as quick as you can."

I knew Daddy was right. I could not let myself go there; after all, I was the one with the name that meant bright light.

CHAPTER SEVEN

Easter 1932 was approaching, and I had just learned in school why Easter was not on the same day every year. Mrs. Wright, my teacher, explained to us that Easter is on the first Sunday, after the first full moon, after the vernal equinox which meant that Easter 1932 fell on March 27th. I was excited about Easter because the church was having a big Easter egg hunt, and we could keep all the eggs we found. I was determined I was going to find plenty and take them home to Momma, so she could eat all that protein and get strong.

I did not get to go to the big Easter egg hunt because Momma took a tragic turn for the worse that Friday before Easter. Her breathing became more and more labored, and Daddy sent for Dr. Bauguess. After checking Momma, he just shook his head. I overheard him telling Daddy that her lungs were full of pneumonia, and there was nothing more he could do.

Daddy, we four kids, and several of the ladies from the church took turns sitting with Momma for the remainder of time she had. Daddy and I were standing vigil when she passed March 27th at

10:00pm. I have never missed anyone more in my life, but I could not dwell on bad thoughts, as Daddy would say. After all, God called Momma home on Easter Sunday, the same day we celebrate Jesus' resurrection. I knew my momma must be really special for God to come and get her on Easter.

CHAPTER EIGHT

The following morning I got up and fixed potato soup and cornbread cakes for breakfast. I had grown tired of all the fried potatoes every morning. One of the ladies from the church, Ms. Ethel, had brought over some fresh milk and freshly churned butter from her cow, Gussy, and we all needed a change.

While I fried those cornbread cakes, I thought about how Momma introduced me to cooking by stirring the cornbread batter and how I watched that batter float around in the hot grease until it sizzled into crisp formed cakes. I felt a little sorry for myself because I was only eleven years old and my momma was gone, but I felt even sorrier for my two sisters, Bonnie and Bessie; after all, Bonnie was only ten and Bessie a tender seven. Daddy was now all alone and my big brother; Will, he needed Momma too. I thought about Momma's stories about how much she wanted me and how she had trained me for this time. I knew I had to be strong now. Momma's saying, "*It's a great life if you don't weaken, but who wants to be strong,*" was taking on a whole new meaning for me.

I went to Momma's apron drawer, pulled out her pink apron trimmed with white tatted lace and tied it around my waist. My position in the family had changed, and now it was my job to take care of them.

I set the table with our best dishes- the white ones with the pretty pink roses in the middle -the very ones Momma always used when the preacher came for Sunday dinner. I called everyone to the breakfast table and even though a word was not spoken that morning, and it is so hard to explain, it was like in our way we were all honoring Momma.

I don't remember much about Momma's wake, but I do remember ironing the dress she was laid out in. I remember that everyone was hugging all of us and crying and saying such nice things about Momma. I remember all the food the church folk brought for us to eat, and Will eating till he was sick because we had survived on little more than potatoes the past few months. The only other memory I have is of seeing Daddy gently touch Momma's hand while tears streamed down his face. I told myself right then that I was going to take good care of Daddy because I needed him now more than ever.

CHAPTER NINE

The weeks following Momma's death were all but erased from my mind. That was God's way of getting me though the initial pain of losing Momma. It was like when you get a really deep cut, and you feel the real bad pain in the beginning, but after some time the pain subsides but you're always left with the scar to remind you of the cut. God carried me though the very worst pain of losing Momma, and when he set me down I was left with the permanent scar on my heart.

By this time, the heat of summer was already setting in. I always knew that Will loved me, but after Momma's passing Will seemed to take me under his wing. Will had Momma's sensitivity and seemed to want to shelter me from any more hurt.

Life got back to some semblance of normalcy again as Daddy got to return to work at the cotton mill. Since it was summertime and we had no school, Bonnie, Bessie and I would take Daddy his lunch every day. The trek was a strenuous one- about a mile long hike with a trip down Cotton Mill Hill going and a trip up Cotton Mill Hill returning home. Bonnie and I thought the trip back home was too strenuous for Little Bessie, and we would lock arms-my right arm to Bonnie's left arm and her right arm to my left. We would then squat so Bessie could sit in our "arm chair" for the walk home. Momma would have been proud that we were all looking after one another.

That same summer I decided it was time for Bonnie to learn to cook. I was going to teach her to make biscuits. I brought her into the kitchen to watch me make biscuit dough. I worked up that dough and sifted flour onto our large cutting board when all at once Will screamed for me. I asked Bonnie to use the rolling pin and roll out the dough while I went to tend to Will, who had just cut his finger with Daddy's axe and needed me to bandage his wound. When I returned to the kitchen, Bonnie was not there and neither was the biscuit dough. I walked out on the porch, and there was Bonnie hitting that dough ball with a stick, and Bessie was running to retrieve it. I screamed out at Bonnie, "You just wasted the most of the flour out of our flour bin, and no man will ever have you if you keep acting like that!"

I decided that just like Momma I would teach Bonnie to make cornbread cakes first; at least, she could not make a ball with that batter.

Bonnie proved to be very stubborn and had no interest in learning to cook or helping with any of the household chores. She was what we called a "tomboy." She had rather be out tending to the animals, helping Daddy and Will in the garden, or digging worms and fishing. I decided it was not worth my energy to try to teach her to cook; I would save my energy for teaching Bessie, who would be old enough soon.

CHAPTER TEN

J ust about the time I got use to life without Momma, Daddy came walking up the hill toward the house with a woman at his side. She looked nothing like Momma. Where Momma was delicate and thin with porcelain skin and long flowing hair, this woman was large and round, with weather-beaten skin and short, wiry hair. I thought that maybe Daddy did not think I was doing a good enough job tending to the family, and he was bringing a hired woman to tend to us.

When Daddy brought her up on the porch I knew he liked this woman because he stood very close to her and hung onto every word that came out of her mouth. Where Momma was quiet, re-served, and very much a lady, she was a loud, boisterous, mountain woman. I could tell by the way Daddy was acting that he wanted me to like her, too. When she did shut her mouth long enough for Daddy to say a word, he looked at me and said, "Lucy, get everyone out here; I have someone I want you to meet."

I went out back to get Will. Bonnie and Bessie were in the house listening to every word this woman said. Bonnie started making kissy faces and mouthing, "She's not going to be my new momma."

I mouthed back, "Behave yourself."

We raced out to meet this woman like a herd of turtles. We would have rather been beat butt naked in front of our enemies than have to go out and meet her. There we stood all in a line on the porch as Daddy cleared his throat and said, "Kids, I want you to meet Bertha."

Bonnie started to snicker, and I gave her a good pinch on the arm to quiet her down. There was an awkward silence for what seemed like forever before Daddy cleared his throat and said, "Bertha, I would like you to meet Will, Lucy, Bonnie, and Bessie."

She looked at us while her hands flattened down the front of her long, brown dress. She shook Will's hand and said, "Pleased to meet you," and then she worked her way down the line.

It reminded me of our mourner's line at Momma's wake. She reached down and hugged me tight, and I noticed that she did not smell anything like Momma. Momma always smelled of fresh lilacs, even when she was sick. This woman smelled like campfire smoke, and even though I was not impressed, I minded my manners. When Bertha reached down to hug Bonnie, Bonnie stiffened her back, and I noticed her arms appeared glued to her sides. Bessie did reciprocate the hug, and then Bertha stood back looking at my daddy and said, "Moe, you have yourself some fine looking kids."

Daddy looked at us as we all just stood there like we were waiting for the next mourner to make his way down the line. With his hand, he shooed us to the front door, "You can get back to your chores now, and I am going to see Bertha home."

We all but ran back in the house and stood peeking out the window as we watched Daddy and Bertha walk back across the hill.

None of us wanted a new momma, especially not "Big Bertha" as Bonnie called her, but I wanted Daddy to be happy, and if "Big Bertha" made him happy, I would try really hard to like her, too. Momma always said, "We can always find something we like in everyone."

I decided that I liked her hugs. Even though I didn't like the way she smelled, she was soft like a goose-down pillow, and she had hugged me like she really meant it.

CHAPTER ELEVEN

I t had not entered my mind until Daddy showed up with Big Bertha that he was looking to get us a new momma. I had settled into my role of taking care of the family pretty nicely. Bessie all but called me Momma and clung to my side most of her waking hours. Daddy and Will frequently complimented my cooking, and even Bonnie said she would take my cooking over Aunt Rouge's any day of the week. Momma had trained me for this time, and I could take care of the family. I didn't see any need for a new momma to come in and upset our little nest.

Around the same time that Daddy showed up with Big Bertha, we were learning about the brain in school. We had just learned that the brain needs lots of protein to keep it functioning properly. Mrs. Wright, my teacher, also stressed to us that meat and eggs were excellent sources of protein. Since the start of the depression, we had been getting most of our protein in our daily diet of potatoes (if that counts as protein) and the occasional egg when our little hen decided to lay one, but meat had been a scarce treat.

After school, Bonnie and I got to talking about Daddy, and we both thought that maybe he was not thinking clearly because his brain lacked protein. We decided that we needed to find Daddy some meat. We knew we could never kill a deer, rabbit, or squirrel and dress it, but Bonnie had the idea that we could trap a bird and prepare it; after all, I had helped Momma kill, de-feather, and dress a couple of chickens in the past. We told Will our idea, and he made us a bird trap. Bonnie and I set up the trap in the woods and waited for half a day until we finally trapped one. We had hoped for a quail or even bigger bird, but the wren we caught would have to do.

I boiled a big pot of water and stuffed that tiny bird into that boiling bath, and before we could get that bird out the kitchen door feathers were flying everywhere. We plucked the last of the feathers from the wren and looked down at the tiny remains. Will saw us hovering over the bird and came to inspect. The exact words out of his mouth were- "There's more protein in a couple of piss ants than that little bird. You might as well quit wasting your time and just sling it over into the woods."

I was not about to do that; after all, we had a lot of time invested in this wren, and Daddy needed protein.

I dressed that little bird like Momma and I dressed those chickens, and I rolled those two small pieces of meat in a flour mixture and fried them on the stove. It really did smell good. I forbade Will, Bonnie, and Bessie from taking a bite; after all, Daddy needed the protein so he could get his head on straight.

When Daddy arrived home from the cotton mill that evening, I already had supper on the table and the two bites of wren meat on his plate. Daddy ate his meat with the usual potatoes, and after dinner, he told us kids that he was going to walk over and see Bertha for a few minutes.

I decided the meat did nothing to clear Daddy's head; it just gave him enough energy to make the trip to Bertha's.

CHAPTER TWELVE

Protein was not curing Daddy's brain problem. He spent more and more time with Bertha. Will overheard Bessie and me talking about Daddy's protein deficiency -how this had impaired his better judgment- and he told us that Daddy did not have a brain problem but a heart problem. He had spied on Daddy kissing Bertha and knew that he was in love with her. It was not long until our whole family was introduced to Bertha Billings' family and her family to ours.

I found out at the time of our big family gathering that Bertha's husband was still living, and she was D-I-V-O-R-C-E-D. She was the first person I ever knew who was divorced. When Bertha and her husband, Bill, parted ways they also divided their two their children with Bertha taking their daughter, Bonnie, and Bill taking their son, Jasper.

I only met Jasper the one time at the big family gathering; he was barely three years old. I remember that he was so small for his age and seemed very frail. He never smiled and appeared heartbroken. He hung onto to the hemline of Bertha's dress the whole day whimpering and crying.

A few months later, I overheard two ladies in the church saying that Jasper had died. They said that he grieved himself to death for Bertha. I could see how that could happen because I missed Momma something fierce, but at least my momma didn't walk off and leave me behind. I could not understand how Bertha could do such a thing; after all, she sure seemed to love her Bonnie.

I had this real unsettled feeling that if she could walk off and leave Jasper, she could talk Daddy into walking off and leaving Will, Bonnie, Bessie, and me behind, as well. I so wanted Daddy to see that we were making it just fine without Bertha, but Daddy was all tangled up in her web, and before we could free him he had up and married "Big Bertha Billings."

CHAPTER THIRTEEN

December 19, 1933- another date forever stamped in my mind. I could not believe my eyes and ears when Daddy entered the house carrying Bertha across the threshold and announcing that they were married. It was the middle of December, for heaven's sakes! What kind of Christmas present was this? We did not ask Santa for a new momma! I just stood there with my mouth wide open like I was trying to catch flies when Bertha patted me on the head and said, "Lucy, go clean out your room and move your stuff in with your other two sisters because my Bonnie will be moving in tomorrow morning, and it's only fair that she has her own room. She has never had sisters before, and this will be a big adjustment for her."

I thought to myself, it's going to be an even bigger adjustment for me, but I did as she asked. I was not really sure that Momma would be happy with this arrangement; after all, she had trained me to take care of the family.

While cleaning out my room, I thought back to Christmas 1931 before Momma died. Daddy's sister-in-law, Eunice, had died suddenly and his brother Floyd brought my three cousins to stay with us so he could go to work in Kentucky. I remembered how sick Momma was and how Uncle Floyd just left our cousins for us to tend to. I know it was just too much for Momma with her being so sick and all, and I know all the added stress played a part in her death.

I myself was not physically sick, but the idea of having a new stepmother and another sister, especially another one named Bonnie, was making me sick. Momma's quote, "*It's a great life if you don't weaken, but who wants to be strong,*" was once again resounding in my mind. I was really starting to understand the message hidden in these words.

I went to the kitchen to fix some cornbread cakes. Cornbread cakes had become a comfort food for me. Making them always made me think of Momma. After the cakes were fried, I called Bonnie and Bessie into the kitchen. While we feasted on those cornbread cakes, I reminded them of the time that Uncle Floyd brought our three cousins to live with us when Momma was so sick. I reminded them of how tenderly and sweetly Momma had treated them, even though she was too sick to be bothered. I told Bonnie and Bessie that even though we did not like this new arrangement we needed to treat Bertha and Bonnie as part of the family because Daddy loved Bertha, Bertha loved her Bonnie, and we girls loved Daddy.

CHAPTER FOURTEEN

Bertha's Bonnie did move in the following day and took over ownership of my room. She, too, was thirteen, but it was immediately obvious that her mother had not properly trained her the way my momma trained me. Bonnie could not cook, iron, or even sweep the floor. The only thing Bonnie could do well was whine. I don't know if she was just plain lazy or if Bertha had just never taught her anything. I felt a renewed sense of pride that I was Ester Elmore's daughter and not Bertha Billings' –well now Bertha Elmore's daughter. (I cringed at the thought of Bertha having my last name.)

We secretly nicknamed Bonnie, "Bonnie Queen Bee," because just like the queen bee in the hive she got to sit around and whine while everyone waited on her hand and foot. Bonnie, Bessie, and I tried to include Bonnie Bee (as we called her for short) in our day to day conversations and activities, but Bonnie Bee mostly clung to Bertha's dress tail. I guess she was afraid Bertha would run off and leave her behind too.

It was soon obvious that Bonnie Bee and Daddy were Bertha's only interests. She was nice enough to Bonnie, Bessie, and me, but much more became required of us Elmore girls.

Will moved out soon after Bertha and Bonnie Bee moved in. He got a job driving the car for Dr. Bauguess who was up in years and had lost his driving privileges. As part of his pay he was granted room and board at the doctor's home.

I sorely missed Will as I had really grown close to him since Momma's death. I figured that once Will moved out that I could take back ownership of my room, but Bertha had other plans for Will's room and made that her official sewing room.

My responsibilities increased after Bertha and Bonnie Bee came to live with us. I kept my cooking duties. I really did not mind that because I had seen Bertha's chicken and dumplings at the big family gathering when our two families met. I remember that big pot of dumplings with the chicken feet floating around on the top. Bonnie, Bessie, and I all stood in amazement around that pot of dumplings with those two yellow chicken feet, with the claws still attached, floating around on top of that dumpling gravy. We made a vow right then to never eat her cooking, so I was grateful that Bertha wanted me to cook. I was also required to take care of all the household chores except for cleaning Bonnie Bee's room and washing her clothes, which Bertha did herself.

Bonnie and Bessie were expected to mind the cows that Bertha brought with her when she married Daddy. Daddy just seemed oblivious to the whole arrangement, and I never complained to him about our new plight.

One day while I was out on the porch washing our clothes, I began thinking about how our lives had transformed into somewhat of a fairy tale. It was like I was actually living the life of Cinderella. I had my ugly stepmother with my lazy stepsister, and I had to cook and clean for the whole family while "Big Bertha" and "Bonnie

Queen Bee" lay around and barked out their orders. I began to giggle and Bonnie Bee asked me what was so funny. I replied, "Oh, nothing," to which she rolled her eyes.

I thought that maybe just like Cinderella, one day my prince would come and I, too, could live happily ever after. I knew I had a better chance than Bonnie "Queen Bee" Billings because I was Ester Elmore's daughter and she had taught me well.

CHAPTER FIFTEEN

Since Momma's death the onset of March always brought a dull ache to my heart, as it conjured up memories of losing Momma, and March of 1935 was no exception. With few sunny days and the temperatures never rising above the high 40's it appeared that spring was taking an extra-long vacation before arriving. All the cold weather had just about depleted Daddy's firewood supply, and we were down to a handful of logs and the wood chips.

On that last March Saturday, Daddy and Bertha decided to make a trip up in the woods above the house and cut up some dead trees lying on the forest floor, as spring was still nowhere in sight. I was doing my Saturday ironing, using a flat iron that I kept hot on the fire. Bonnie Bee was doing her usual sitting and whining. She was extra whiney because Bertha had given her strict orders to stay inside because she seemed to be coming down with a cold. Bertha also gave me instructions to take care of Bonnie Bee while she and Daddy went to get wood. Bonnie and Bessie were off minding the cows down at the creek.

After Bertha and Daddy left, I decided to give my arms a break from that heavy iron and sat down to read a few chapters in my newly acquired book, <u>Mary Poppins,</u> by P. L. Travers. I loved to read because it was my only escape. I could venture anywhere in a book and live through those characters. Mary Poppins reminded me a lot of Bertha, and I imagined that I was one of the Banks children. I could not decide if I liked Mary Poppins or not- parts of her I did like and parts I did not like so well. It was exactly like my ordeal with Bertha. There were things about Bertha I did like and other things about her that left a real sour taste in my mouth. I was totally absorbed in the book when, all at once, I heard the wood stove door slam shut. I jolted back to reality and looked up to find Bonnie Bee walking back across the sitting room. I asked her what she was doing and she replied, "The fire was dying out, and I just tossed all those wood chips into the stove."

I told her that she should not have done that because those were pine chips, and they were full of rosin.

She just looked at me and said, "What's done is done," as she wiped her nose on her sleeve.

I went back to reading my book, but after a few minutes I was again interrupted by a roaring sound in the chimney. I put my book aside and went outside to see if I could tell what was going on, and I could not believe my eyes. Fire and smoke were billowing out of the chimney. I saw those fiery embers lighting on the roof, and then I heard Bonnie Bee scream.

I ran back inside and saw that smoke was filling the sitting room. I screamed at Bonnie Bee to get out of the house. She just stood there coughing and rubbing her eyes. I ran over and grabbed her by the arm and pulled her out into the yard. By this time, I could see that the roof had caught fire, and I just knew our house was burning down.

I remembered that Momma's trunk was in the house, and I could not stand to lose that to fire because it held all the earthly remnants of my momma. That trunk housed the letters she wrote each of us kids before she died, her wedding dress, pieces of her jewelry, a lock of her hair, her Bible, and pictures of Momma and our Elmore family. I ran back into the house. Through all the heavy smoke, I saw the trunk at the bottom of the staircase. I hollered at Bonnie Bee to come and help me drag it out. Before she made it back inside, I had dragged that trunk myself out onto the porch. Bonnie Bee helped me drag it on out into the yard, and we stood there for what seemed like forever watching our house burn down.

Suddenly, I remembered that Bonnie and Bessie were down at the creek minding the cows. I did not want them to walk up over the hill and see that our house was burning down, as I thought that might just put them into shock. I ran as fast as my legs would carry me down to the creek. They were not in the usual spot where they watered the cows, and I began to panic. I continued to follow the path by the creek, until I heard Bessie laughing and Bonnie screaming, "Shut up, it's not funny!"

As Bonnie came into view, I witnessed her trying to wipe the fresh cow manure from the top of her shoe with dried leaves and a stick. Bessie and Bonnie saw me and immediately knew something was bad wrong. Bonnie stood straight up, throwing the manure covered leaves and stick down, and Bessie screamed, "Oh, Lucy, what's wrong?"

The words were frozen in my throat, and all I could get out was a faint whisper, "The house is on fire, and it is burning to the ground!"

Bessie and Bonnie immediately burst into tears. Before any one of us could give it a second thought, we went running back to our homeplace leaving Bertha's cows behind.

By the time we got home, Daddy and Bertha were pulling up into the drive. Daddy jumped out of the truck and said, "Lord, have mercy on us all. What just happened?"

I explained that I heard an awful roar in the chimney. When I went to check it, the chimney was on fire and shooting embers all over the roof. Bertha immediately looked over at Bonnie Bee and said, "Honey, are you ok?"

Bonnie Bee began to whimper and cry, and Bertha just sat right down on that cold ground and held Bonnie Bee on her lap, rocking her back and forth. We Elmore girls just stood there all huddled together, and Bertha never bothered to ask us if we were ok.

It seemed like we stood there for an eternity when Bertha blurted out, "Oh, Bonnie, you saved my trunk!"

I shifted around to take a look myself, and I could not believe what I was seeing. It was indeed Bertha's trunk! I had pulled Bertha's trunk from the fire! I could feel the tears stinging my eyes, but I refused to allow myself to cry. I wanted to scream, "That was supposed to be Momma's trunk! That was all we had left of her!" Instead, I just stood there and did not open my mouth.

I thought that maybe Bertha had some of Jasper's belongings in her trunk that she needed to keep after giving him up so easy and him up and dying so young. I decided to hold onto that thought; Bertha needed that trunk because she needed to hold onto Jasper. I was glad that I saved Jasper for her.

I knew that even though all Momma's earthly possessions had burned up in the fire, I was still Ester Elmore's daughter, and no fire could destroy all the memories of her that I held deep in my heart.

CHAPTER SIXTEEN

M arch 30, 1935 the day our house burned changed my life even more than March 27, 1932 the day my momma died. I was beginning to think that March must be my bad luck month. That night we stayed in the little apartment above the garage of our neighbor, Jack Swift. He told my daddy we could stay there until the house could be rebuilt.

The apartment only had two bedrooms, and all four of us girls had to sleep in the same bed. Bonnie Bee cried half the night and complained of being too cramped with hot breath pouring down on her every way she turned. I could see that unless something changed none of us would get any sleep.

I crawled out of bed and made a pallet with two quilts on the floor. I asked if anyone wanted to sleep with me, and Bessie hopped off that bed and onto that hard, cold floor with me. Bessie snuggled up against me and asked if I would tell her a happy story. I liked the feel of Bessie's warmth against my back, as it made me feel safe. Even though we did not have our home, we still had each other, and as long as we were together as a family everything would be ok.

I took in a deep breath and began the whispered story: "Once upon a time there was farmer who had a young daughter. She was the most beautiful girl in all the land with soft blonde hair and rosy red cheeks. Why, she looked just like you Bessie; in fact, her name was Bessie. The farmer loved his daughter and wanted more than anything for her to find true happiness. He knew that if she married a prince and they had a castle full of children she would be forever happy. One morning the farmer set out with his prized cow to find a prince for his Bessie."

I could hear Bessie begin to snore to which I whispered, "and they lived happily ever after."

I fluffed my pillow, snuggled under the quilt, and closed my eyes for some much needed sleep. I was awakened the following morning by the voices of Daddy and Bertha. I overheard Bertha telling Daddy that the apartment was way too small for all six of us, and since I was the oldest other arrangements needed to be made for me.

I felt a jolt of terror shoot through my body. Was Bertha saying that I should leave like Will did? Will was almost seventeen when he left home, and he was ready to leave since he had a job and a girlfriend. I was still 4 months away from being fifteen, and I did not have a job or even a boyfriend. I decided that I would cook an extra good breakfast, and even though it was Sunday, I would take to my chores without any instruction. I would make them see that they needed to keep me.

I got up quietly, so not to disturb Bonnie, Bessie and Bonnie Bee, as they were still asleep. I dressed in the same clothes from Saturday, as they were the only ones that did not burn up in the fire. I then tiptoed into the kitchen and found fresh eggs and canned sausage that Jack had left for us. I opened the can of sausage and fried it out until it was brown and crispy. I, then, fried those eggs in the sausage grease, making sure that the yolks were unbroken, and the egg whites contained no lace- or scabs- as Bessie called it.

By the time breakfast was cooked, Bonnie, Bessie, and Bonnie Bee were all up and sitting at the table. Daddy and Bertha joined us as we sat down to eat. Before we began eating, Daddy asked all of us to bow our heads for grace. I will never forget part of that prayer for those words are forever stamped in my mind. He cleared his throat and in a trembled voice said: *"Lord, I want to pray a special blessing on my sweet Lucy. She is our bright light and no matter where life takes her, please be with her, Dear Jesus, and keep your light shining in her heart."*

I could hardly eat a bite that morning because I could not get the food past the big lump that had lodged in the back of my throat. I knew that Bertha had sealed my fate, and it would not be long until I, too, would be left behind just like Jasper. I decided not to dwell on that, after all it was a bad thought, and Daddy always said that if you have a bad thought get it out of your mind as quick as you can.

CHAPTER SEVENTEEN

That same evening, while I went out back to sling the dirty dish water over the hill, I heard a car pulling into the driveway. When I walked around front, I could see that it was Daddy's sister, Aunt Pandy, and her husband, Uncle Albert. I didn't know why they would bother stopping by now. Aunt Pandy hardly ever showed her face during Momma's sickness and never did anything to help us as far as I could tell. At Momma's wake, she made up some excuse to Daddy about her kids and Uncle Albert keeping her so busy that she never had any time to just sit down and enjoy the light of day. I figured that plain old nosiness was what brought them here. They wanted to see the pile of ashes that lay on the ground where our house once stood.

Daddy met Aunt Pandy and Uncle Albert out front, and he saw me making my way out to where they stood talking. He looked at me and said, "Lucy, you go ahead and get yourself back in the house."

I did as I was told.

I walked back into the bedroom that all four of us shared, and I peeked out the window down onto Daddy, Aunt Pandy, and Uncle Albert. They were obviously talking about something very important because Daddy was wringing his hands, something he always did when he was nervous. Aunt Pandy was standing with her hands firmly fastened to the sides of her hips, and Uncle Albert was scratching one of his chins. I could count three chins from my window view. I couldn't help but giggle at that, but I could also feel that big lump making its way back up my throat. I remembered Daddy and Bertha's conversation from this morning and Daddy's prayer at breakfast -the part about me- "no matter where life takes her…."

I knew in my heart that they were discussing my fate; why else would Daddy have told me to get back inside? I closed my eyes tight and thought back to those times before I lost Momma. I could see plain as day in my mind, Momma in her pretty blue dress holding me tight to her chest and singing my song while she gently stroked my hair. With my eyes still closed tight, I began to softly hum and then sing those lyrics myself:

My baby Lucy with hair of blonde and eyes of blue
I know you will grow up to be honest and true
Where ever life takes you be it close or far away
I will love my little Lucy till my dying day.

When I opened my eyes, the lump was gone from my throat, and I felt a kind of warmth and peace enveloping me. I knew that whatever my fate, God had blessed me with a photographic memory of my time spent with Momma, and I could call on these memories to calm me whenever times got hard.

CHAPTER EIGHTEEN

I knew when I saw Daddy slowly walking up the steps still wringing his hands, and Aunt Pandy and Uncle Albert not getting into their car to leave but standing like statues out in the yard that life as I had known it was about to change again. One thing was for sure; my momma had helped to make me strong because I could roll with the punches.

I remember Daddy walking in the door and calling, "Lucy, I need to see you."

I took in a deep breath, collected my composure, and went into the sitting room where Daddy stood. He looked down at me, and a huge tear welled up in the corner of his eye. For a few seconds he just stood there looking at me, and then he began to speak, "Lucy, I want you to go and stay with your Aunt Pandy and Uncle Albert. They want you to come and help them take care of the house and kids. This apartment is so small, and we just don't have room. I know you can handle this Lucy because you are strong and hardworking. Why, you are the spitting image of your momma."

He reached down to stroke my hair, but I grabbed him around the neck and hugged him tight. He hugged me back and whispered in my ear, "I love you, Lucy."

I tried to say those words back, but they got stuck in my throat around that ever forming lump. I could feel the tears welling in the corner of my eyes, but I refused to release them. I just continued to hold to his neck for the longest time, and then I let my arms go limp.

I tried to make him feel ok about his decision by saying, "Well, Daddy, it's ok, you and Momma got married when she was fifteen, and I am just four months shy of that now. It's better for me to go than Bonnie or Bessie because neither one of them can tend to young'uns' or cook a lick."

The one good thing about this whole ordeal was that I did not have to pack a bag because the only possessions I now owned were the clothes covering my body.

I went out back to find Bessie and Bonnie and tell them bye. Bessie started crying. She held to my arm and begged me not to leave. I tried to comfort her telling her that it would not be for long, even though, in my mind, I knew Bertha would never allow me back home. I tried to add a spring to my step and appear cheerful as I made my way out to the waiting car. I didn't want Daddy, Bonnie, and Bessie to worry about me, but I wanted them to see that I was ok.

I opened the door to the car and crawled in. Aunt Pandy immediately began talking about what a big help I would be around the house and how I could help to take much of the load off from her. I knew I was in for some tough times ahead, but I knew in my heart that I would be ok because as Daddy said, I was the spitting image of my momma.

CHAPTER NINETEEN

The quote by Friedrich Nietzsche, "*What does not kill you makes you stronger,*" pretty much summed up the period of time that I lived with Aunt Pandy and Uncle Albert. That evening after we got to Aunt Pandy's and Uncle Albert's, Aunt Pandy took me in and showed me to my room while Uncle Albert went to pick up my cousins, Estelle, Ennis, and Agnes.

My room was situated in the far corner off the back porch of the house. It was very small and dark with one tiny window facing west. I think it was intended to be a food pantry. The room was furnished with a small twin bed, a nightstand, and a foot locker. One thing was for sure, I now had a room of my own because only one person could fit in the room.

Aunt Pandy handed me a bag, and I looked inside to find a secondhand dress and some underclothes. She said the clothes were for me. I thanked her, and then she added that she also had some material that I could use to make myself a new dress. I had never made any clothes. I had re-attached the occasional button and darned socks, but Momma got too sick and died before teaching me that skill. I told Aunt Pandy that I would love to learn to sew. She told me that she would teach me after I completed all my daily chores. She stressed that I must complete ALL my daily chores before having any free time. I asked her what my daily chores would be, and she said that we would get to that in the morning after sending my three cousins off to school. I looked up at her and asked, "Can I not go to school?"

She stared down at me and said, "I really can't see any sense in you going back to school."

I could not believe what I was hearing. I loved school and had almost completed the eighth grade. I hesitated for a moment and then in my softest, sweetest voice I said, "But I would really like to go to school. We only have two more months and I will be through the eighth grade. I will work extra hard before school and after school to complete my chores if I can please finish this year."

She glared at me with piercing eyes, while pointing her bony finger in my face, and said, "Let me tell you something, Miss Lucy, I myself only went to the fifth grade, and a girl doesn't need too much education because she is liable to get above her raising."

I thought to myself, but I did not dare say it out loud," Why, if you didn't know, I am Ester Elmore's daughter, and I could never top that nor would I want to."

She turned and walked back into the kitchen without saying another word. I opened the footlocker and placed the dress and underclothes inside and sat down on my new bed. I could see the sun setting through the small window. I took in a deep breath and let out a sigh. I had not been here thirty minutes and it already seemed an eternity. I already missed Daddy, Bessie, and Bonnie; in fact, I was so homesick I would have been glad to see Bertha and Bonnie Bee.

I lay back on my bed and had just closed my eyes when I heard Uncle Albert pulling up into the driveway. I heard all three of my cousins come barreling through the door and straight to my room. There stood Estelle, Ennis, and Agnes looking at me like I was some kind of alien. I smiled and said, "Is there anything the matter?"

Agnes, who was six, walked over to the edge of the bed and stood facing me. She put her hands around her mouth and whispered, "Did your house burn all the way into the ground?"

My eleven year old cousin, Estelle, pinched Agnes on the arm and said, "You're not supposed to say anything about that." Agnes jerked her arm from Estelle's grip and said, "Ouch! I'm going to tell Momma!"

As Agnes ran to tattle on Estelle, nine year old Ennis said, "Is it true that you don't have anything left? Did you only get out with the hair on your head?"

I was so tired and numb that I could not even respond. It was like I was in a tunnel, and the harder I tried to escape the longer and darker that tunnel got. My eyes were so heavy that I could hardly keep them open. I just wanted to lie down, go to sleep, and dream of Momma. Estelle sensed my grief and said, "Come on Ennis; let's leave her alone."

When they left the room, I lay back on my bed and noticed the room was almost pitch black. There was no overhead light or lantern to chase away the dark, so I just lay there anticipating what was coming next. I could hear muffled voices in the sitting room and, after a few minutes, I heard the sound of footsteps coming closer to my room. It was Aunt Pandy. She stuck her head in my door and said, "You can go ahead and get ready for bed because I expect you up at 6:00am."

She added, "Good night, and don't forget to say your prayers."

I took off my clothes, leaving on my underclothes, and crawled into bed. This was the first time in months that I had a bed to myself, and how I wished I could be back in the little apartment in that bed with my sisters and Bonnie Bee. I pulled the covers up around my neck, closed my eyes, and prayed this selfish prayer:

"God, you know my momma wanted me more than anything on earth, and she named me Lucy which means bringer of light. Well, I am trying real hard to live up to my name, but I need some help from you and Momma. You know that Momma's real special God because you came and got her on Easter. Well, I need a real big favor from you....I need you to let Momma visit me tonight in my dreams because I am about as sad and lonely as I can get. I really need for her to hug me tight and tell me that everything is going to be ok. It's in your name I pray. Amen."

I never opened my eyes again after that prayer. I began to hum my song and think about Momma, and before I knew it I had drifted to sleep.

CHAPTER TWENTY

I was now completely and totally convinced that God was real because he answered my prayer. Through my dreams last night God had allowed me the sweetest visit with my momma. She and I were walking down by the river, and it was spring time. The flowers were blooming, and I could even smell the lilacs and wisteria in the air. Momma was holding my hand, and we were talking when all of a sudden she told me she was going to teach me to fly. While still holding to my hand, we began to skip and then run when a gentle breeze blew under us and lifted us off the ground. Momma told me to pump my feet up and down, and we could go higher. With her hand still firmly gripping mine, we pumped our feet, gaining altitude, until we landed on a big fluffy cloud drifting across the sky. I could see the river and grass below me and the sun shining brightly above me. We lay back on the cloud and let the sun pour its warming rays over us. I have never felt so much warmth and peace.

Momma began to sing my song, and I lay my head on her chest while she gently stroked my hair. We drifted on that cloud the

longest time, neither of us wanting to leave because it felt too perfect. I sensed I was going to have to leave, and I kissed Momma's
cheek. She, then, kissed my forehead and held me tight while saying, "Lucy, I love you. I love you so much."

I could not get out the words to reciprocate fast enough. "I love
you too, Momma, I love you so, so much."

I awoke with those words still on my lips.

When I opened my eyes, Aunt Pandy was standing in the doorway telling me that it was time to get up. I smiled at her and said,
"Good Morning."

She did not return the pleasantry but told me that I could
get washed up with the bucket of water that was sitting on the
back porch. I got up and opened my footlocker, revealing the
clothes Aunt Pandy had given me. I took off my underclothes
and replaced them with the fresh ones. I then pulled the dress
over my head and noticed that it was way too big. It was practically hanging off my body. I thought to myself, I really am
Cinderella, but I knew that in due time, I, too, would get my
prince.

I walked out onto the porch. I found the water bucket, but I
could not find a clean rag to use, so I just dipped my hands into
the cold water and splashed my face. Before going back into the
house, I closed my eyes and whispered a prayer:

*"Thank you God for letting Momma visit me last night. I know
you heard and answered my prayer. As Daddy prayed yesterday, I,
too, want you to keep Jesus shining in my heart and always help me,
Dear Lord, I pray. Amen"*

I walked back inside to the kitchen to find Aunt Pandy cooking
eggs and grits. She said, "Your daddy says you're a real good
cook."

I replied, "I have been cooking since I was eight."

She responded, "I just hate to cook, so starting in the morning, I am going to let you take over, and we can see for ourselves how good you are."

I thought, this must be a test to see if they are going to keep me?

Ennis, Estelle, and Agnes came into the kitchen all dressed for school followed by Uncle Albert. My three cousins sat on the long bench that ran alongside the table. Uncle Albert took his place at the head of the table. Aunt Pandy turned to serve Uncle Albert his plate of grits and eggs, and spied me still standing in the doorway. Aunt Pandy pointed her bony finger to the spot on the bench that was closet to Uncle Albert and said, "Lucy, you can take a seat there."

I walked over and took my seat. I could feel my dress sliding off one of my shoulders, and I kept working trying to keep it up. Uncle Albert took notice, too, and smiled at me, but I just couldn't smile back. I could feel his eyes fixed on me, but I kept my eyes fixed on Aunt Pandy. She next served Agnes, Ennis, and Estelle their plates, and then placed her own plate on the table before serving me. I could not help but notice that everyone but me had a decent sized portion on their plate. It really didn't matter because my stomach did not feel like taking in too much.

When Aunt Pandy sat down, Uncle Albert looked up and told us all to bow our heads as he literally exploded into prayer. He started out in a normal voice, but soon his voice grew louder and louder with the words coming out faster and faster like he was being wound up or something. I could feel little pellets of spit hitting on my hand and face, and I could not help but lift my head a little and peek. Uncle Albert's face was all red with those three chins flapping against his neck and the top of his head was sweating something fierce. I thought he just might burst right here at this table. I got tickled at the thought and knew I dare not laugh out loud, so I just started thinking about Momma until I heard him say, "Amen."

After breakfast, Agnes, Ennis, and Estelle left for school, and Uncle Albert went to work. I was left alone with Aunt Pandy. I watched as Aunt Pandy collected the breakfast dishes, scraping them clean into the bowl containing the egg shells. She instructed me to sling the scraps out to the chickens while she gathered her hat and water bucket. I took the bowl out the back door and, keeping my grip firm to its handle, I slung the contents of the bowl out into the yard. I stood and watched as the chickens began pecking at those scraps.

I went back inside and found Aunt Pandy waiting on me. She handed me one of her sweaters and told me to put it on because she was taking me down to the spring to show me where to fetch water. We walked at least a half-mile downhill to the spring. When we got down to the creek there was an actual black pipe sticking out of its bank, through which the spring water ran. It emptied into a permanent wooden box that had been built inside the creek to keep milk and other cold food items. Aunt Pandy placed the bucket under the pipe until it was filled with the cold spring water and then instructed me to pick it up and carry it back to the house.

The walk back was grueling. It was so hard to try to climb back up that hill without slipping on the leaves all the while managing that heavy bucket. Several times, I stumbled, and that icy cold water splashed out onto my legs and feet, almost taking my breath.

When we returned to the house, Aunt Pandy told me to heat some of the water on the wood stove, and then clean up the breakfast dishes while she went and gathered the dirty clothes. I cleaned the dishes and even swept up the floor without her instruction.

Aunt Pandy then told me to gather my dirty clothes and tie them all together because we were taking another hike down to the spring. I asked Aunt Pandy why we were taking our dirty clothes to the spring.

She responded, "Monday is wash day at this house and you, Miss Lucy, are now responsible for washing the clothes and hanging them out to dry."

I already had experience with doing laundry but not the way Aunt Pandy did it. I think Uncle Albert must have been too stingy to buy her a wringer washing machine because we hauled all that laundry along with a tub and scrub board down to the creek. I helped Aunt Pandy gather wood to build a fire, and we boiled those clothes over the fire in the tub we had carried with us. Aunt Pandy handed me some lye soap, and I rubbed those clothes with the soap while scrubbing them on a washboard. After scrubbing all those clothes, we placed them back into that boiling water, stirring them around with a stick before fishing them out. Once the clothes were cool enough, we wrung them with our bare hands. We emptied the wash tub of the water and placed the clean clothes along with the scrubbing board and soap inside. Aunt Pandy grabbed one side of the tub and I the other and we made our second grueling trip back up to the house.

By the time we got back, Estelle, Agnes, and Ennis were already in from school. We dropped the wash tub on the porch, and Aunt Pandy told me to hang the clothes out on the line. After I had finished I felt that I might drop; after all, I had not eaten since breakfast and that was only the few bites that Aunt Pandy put on my plate.

I went into the kitchen and found Ennis, Estelle, Agnes, along with Aunt Pandy eating cold bread and molasses. I knew Aunt Pandy could tell I was hungry because she handed me the one bite of biscuit she had left and told me to pour myself a glass of water. I was so hungry I took the bite of biscuit and all but swallowed it whole. I poured myself a glass of water, and when Aunt Pandy and my cousins left the kitchen I licked every crumb of biscuit off the plate.

I remembered the chickens pecking out in the yard for those meager scraps this morning, and I thought, I might end up like those chickens pecking around for every bite I get.

CHAPTER TWENTY-ONE

I went to bed that night as tired as I had ever been. I think I was asleep before my head hit the pillow, and it did not seem like any time before I heard Aunt Pandy telling me it was time to get up again. When I rolled over to crawl out of bed, I could feel every muscle in my body scream out in pain. I slowly pulled myself up onto my feet and got dressed. I went out onto the back porch and washed up before making my way into the kitchen. I thought, today is my test to see if they keep me.

I went into the kitchen, and Aunt Pandy gave me my orders to cook the eggs and sausage she had out on the counter. I fixed the sausage and eggs just like I did at home, except I used the sausage remnants to make cream gravy. I also made a pan of soft, fluffy biscuits just like Momma taught me. Everyone made their way to the table and took their usual seats. I did not fix everyone a plate like Aunt Pandy but set the food in bowls in the middle of the kitchen table. I sat down at my designated spot and waited for grace. Uncle Albert did not pray with the intensity and fervor that he had yesterday but simply blessed the food and then said, "Let's dig in!"

Uncle Albert grabbed the plate of sausage and began piling it on his plate when Aunt Pandy said, "Albert, you start, and then pass it to me, and I will pass it on around the table."

I was sitting on Uncle Albert's right so that meant I would be the last served again. By the time the food had made its way around the table, there was one biscuit and a spoonful of gravy left. I grabbed the biscuit and what gravy was left. I was so hungry that eating that biscuit only made me crave more. When Uncle Albert finished eating the huge pile he had loaded onto his plate he looked at me and said, "Lucy, you can cook real good," all the while rubbing his swollen belly that hung over his pants.

Ennis, Estelle, and Agnes also bragged on my cooking. I think Aunt Pandy was a little jealous because she just said, "Well, I guess you cook a little better than common for a girl your age."

I got up to clear the table, and Uncle Albert patted me on the shoulder as he was walking out the door. "Lucy, I like how you cook. Yeah, I think I like the idea of keeping you around."

When the kitchen cleared, I started to scrape the plates into the bowl with the egg shells, but I was still so hungry I decided to eat what scraps remained and let the chickens fend for themselves today.

CHAPTER TWENTY-TWO

L ife at Aunt Pandy's and Uncle Albert's never got any easier. I
went to bed every night dog tired. I now knew why Aunt Pandy
had offered to help me make a dress after I completed all my daily
chores. She knew she would never have to bother teaching me
to sew because after completing ALL my chores each day it was
bedtime. The only day I had some free time was on Sunday after-
noons. Aunt Pandy said it was bad luck to sew on Sunday, so she
had all the excuses she needed.

Uncle Albert was never around much, but when he was he
made me feel uncomfortable. Just the way he looked at me made
my skin crawl.

About four months after I moved in with Aunt Pandy, I heard
footsteps making their way toward my bedroom one night after
everyone had gone to bed. I knew it was Uncle Albert because
I had learned the sound of everyone's footsteps, with my bedroom being off the back porch, and the outhouse just a few feet
away from the house. I assumed he was going out for his nightly
visit, but instead of going out the back door I heard him moving

toward my room. I could not see a thing, but I could feel his presence in the doorway. A moment later I heard him whisper, "Lucy, are you asleep?"

I gave no response; I lay there with my eyes tightly shut and prayed that he would go away.

Again, he said, "Lucy, are you asleep?"

I remained still as a mouse, and then I felt him place his hand on top of my bed covers and begin to pull them back. About that same time, I heard Aunt Pandy get out of bed and start shuffling down the hall. Uncle Albert heard it too because he quickly left my room and headed off to the outhouse.

The next morning, after everyone was out of the house, and Aunt Pandy and I were all that remained, I told her about Uncle Albert coming to my room. Quick as a flash, she slapped me hard across my face and said, "You liar!"

I was shocked, mad, hurt, confused- every feeling imaginable all rolled up together. I did not say another word to Aunt Pandy. I gathered myself and walked back into the kitchen to start my chores.

Around midday, Aunt Pandy came out onto the back porch as I was weeding her truck garden. She sat down all holier than thou and began reading her Bible. I continued to work, not paying her any mind, when all at once I heard her say, "Lucy, do you have something you need to say to me?"

I looked up and said, "I don't know what you mean."

She replied, "I think you owe me an apology."

I didn't open my mouth.

She raised her voice at least three octaves, "You need to tell me you are sorry about that lie you told this morning."

I still did not respond.

I heard her slam her Bible shut and walk back into the house. I did not understand why she would not believe me, but that night I wrote a letter to Daddy asking him to let me come back home.

It would be a month before I heard back from Daddy and life during that time became more and more unbearable. Every night before I went to bed I put every stitch of clothing I owned on my body, and I slept with one eye open. I could not even go fetch water without worrying about Uncle Albert hiding in the woods.

The day before I heard back from Daddy I was down at the spring just finishing up the wash when I heard twigs breaking up in the woods. I just knew it was Uncle Albert, and I started to gather everything as fast as I could. Just as I started up the hill, I saw him coming after me. He was telling me to wait, but I knew better. I was so tired from my chores that I had no energy left to run. I was praying that God would just see me back to the house when all at once I slipped and fell, spilling my load of laundry down the hill. Uncle Albert slipped on one of the bed sheets and fell as well.

I managed to make it back up to the house, but Aunt Pandy was gone. I ran back to my room and slammed the door shut. A minute later I heard Uncle Albert get into his truck and drive off. I knew I had to get back down the hill and gather all those clothes up and rewash them before Aunt Pandy returned home, but I had no strength left in my body. I laid back on my bed for a few minutes before finally making my way back down the hill. As I gathered up all those clothes that now lay soiled on the ground, I prayed:

"God, I really need your help now more than any other time in my life. I am trying so hard to keep my bright light shining but I am so, so tired. Keep me safe and strong and please find a way to let Daddy know what is happening to me. I know if he knew what I was going through he would talk to Bertha and see a way to get me back home. I need him to come get me now before it's too late. And always help me, Dear Lord, I pray, Amen."

That night I decided to even wear my shoes to bed, that way if Uncle Albert bothered me I could kick him where it hurt, and Aunt Pandy could see for herself that I was no liar.

CHAPTER TWENTY-THREE

I woke up the next morning feeling real bad. I didn't think I could manage the breakfast smells without getting sick all over the place. On my way to the kitchen I just whispered under my breath, *"Help me, Dear Lord I pray"*.

I passed Aunt Pandy in the doorway, as she was heading to the outhouse. She looked at me and asked, "What's the matter, Lucy?"

I told her I felt real bad and my stomach was cramping something fierce.

She just pointed that old bony finger at me and said, "You need not try your excuses with me. Now get on in there and fix breakfast."

I did as she requested, but when we all assembled at the breakfast table I left my plate empty. After breakfast Uncle Albert left for work, and Aunt Pandy said that she was going to her women's meeting down at the First United Holiness Church of Jesus Christ.

Since Estelle, Ennis, and Agnes were out of school for the summer, I would be in charge to look after them. As soon as everyone was out of the house, I asked Estelle, who had just turned 12, if she would scrape the breakfast dishes and sweep the floor because I just had to go lie down for a minute. She looked up at me and said, "Lucy, why do you always work so hard? You never go out and play with us. Why, if I didn't know any better I would think you were our slave."

I was taken aback by her words. I stood there for a minute and collected my response before speaking. Momma had always told me to measure twice and cut once. I didn't want Estelle to have reason to think poorly of her parents so I just said, "Your momma needs my help, and I'm real glad to help her."

Estelle replied, "Lucy, I would never tell Momma this, but you're a real good cook, much better than her. I wish you'd teach me sometime."

I told her that I just might do that, but right now I needed to go lie down. I must have fallen sound asleep because I was startled awake by Aunt Pandy screaming my name. I sat straight up on my bed, rubbed my eyes, and pulled back the strands of hair from my face. I walked out to the sitting room where Aunt Pandy stood.

She snarled, "You got a letter from your daddy."

My heart began racing. I reached for the letter and thanked her, as I took it from her hand. I hurried back to my room, closed the door behind me, plopped down on my bed, and ripped the envelope open. I unfolded the letter as quick as I could. Before I read a single word, I just scanned all the letters on the paper. I had never seen my daddy's handwriting before, and I thought to myself, the words on this paper were written by my daddy. This was the closest I had felt to home in almost five months. I took in a deep breath and began to read:

Dear Lucy,
I know you want to come home real bad. Well, I have some good news and bad news. The bad news is that I really can't bring you home right now. We are moving out to Virginia because I got a job

in Kentucky, in a little town called Jenkins, just across the state line. I will be working in the coal mine, and the pay is real good so maybe one day but just not now. The good news is that I am sending Bessie down to Pandy and Albert's to stay with you. She has grieved over you something terrible since you've been away. She's becoming a puny little thing, and we don't think the move would be good for her. Anyway, it was real good hearing from you. I love you, and take care of yourself, Lucy.
Daddy

I could not believe what I was reading. Did Daddy not even read my letter? How could he say it was real good hearing from me when I told him about Uncle Albert? I knew that Daddy could not have seen my letter or written me back. Bertha had intercepted my letter and never said a word to Daddy. Bertha had written the letter, and those were her words on the paper! I ripped that letter to shreds and threw it in the trashcan.

I was happy that Bessie was coming, but now I would have her to protect from Albert, too. (I had decided to never use Uncle in front of his name, ever again, because after what he had done to me he did not deserve that respect.)

CHAPTER TWENTY-FOUR

L ate that same evening, I went into the kitchen and without Aunt Pandy's permission I began to fry myself a cornbread cake. I had not made cornbread cakes since I left home. Aunt Pandy only kept a handful of meal on hand because Albert could not grow it in his garden, and he thought it too expensive to buy. After getting that letter from Daddy, or should I say Bertha, I needed a touch from Momma. Frying that cake the way she taught me, took me right back home.

After the cornbread cake was fried, I sat right down at the table and began to eat it. Aunt Pandy came into the kitchen and saw what I was doing. In a bitter voice, she said, "Did you use my meal?"

I swallowed the bite of cornbread cake before replying, "Well, yes, but just a little."

She glared her piercing gray eyes at me and said, "I ought to just slap that right out of your mouth."

Before I thought, I said, "Well, it would not be the first time."

To which she retorted, "The Bible says: *Thou shalt not steal.*"

I knew I could never win this fight so I just said, "I'm sorry Aunt Pandy, it will never happen again."

Aunt Pandy stomped out of the kitchen, and I finished eating my cornbread cake, savoring every bite. I cleaned up my dishes and went on back to my room. It was almost dark, and I was sleepy. I got into bed and pulled the covers all the way up to my neck. I thought, for the first time in five months I am not going to bed hungry, and I am not sorry for that.

CHAPTER TWENTY-FIVE

B essie arrived one week after I got my letter. When I saw Albert's car pulling into the driveway, I could hardly wait for Bessie to get out so I could throw my arms around her neck and tell her how glad I was to see her. She must have been thinking the same thing because she jumped out of Albert's car before it even came to a complete stop. She made a beeline for me, almost knocking me down, as she reached up and grabbed my neck. She just burst out crying, and I couldn't hold the tears back either. We stood there for the longest time just hugging and looking at each other.

I took immediate notice, that just like the letter said, Bessie had become a puny little thing. I remembered Bertha's chicken and dumplings, and I thought Bertha's cooking must taste as bad as it looked because Bessie looked like she was wasting away.

Aunt Pandy allowed me to show Bessie around. I showed her my room and told her that it would be her room, too. I had decided after I got the letter that Bessie would sleep with me no matter how much Aunt Pandy and Albert protested. I was determined that Bessie would not suffer at the hand of Albert like I had.

Momma had always said, "It's a poor hen that can't look after one little chicken," and I was going to take care of Bessie if I had to fight tooth and nail.

That night we crawled into the tiny bed together. We couldn't help but giggle because it was all we could do to both stay on and not fall out into the floor. When we finally got situated, I whispered, "Bessie, I love you, and I'm really glad you're with me."

Bessie responded with, "I love you too, Lucy," as she wrapped her arm around my shoulder and squeezed tight.

I thought back to that last night we spent together on the apartment floor and how safe I felt that night with Bessie all scrooched up to me. I smiled at the thought and said, "Bessie, do you want to hear a happy story?"

She squealed, "More than anything."

I started: "Once upon a time......" and before I knew it, both of us were sound asleep.

CHAPTER TWENTY-SIX

B essie filled me in on everything that had happened at home since I left, and things had changed a lot. According to Bessie, Bonnie had been farmed out to the Wilson's who lived down in Thurmond. She was being paid one dollar a week, but she had to send half of her earnings back home. I thought that was all Bertha's idea because I knew Daddy would never hire Bonnie out and then take away her money. I had never made one dime working for Aunt Pandy and Albert, but at the same time I would rather not get paid than to have to send it to Bertha.

Bessie said that Bonnie Bee was still her whiney self, and she knew that she really got on Daddy's nerves because he would sit in his chair at night wringing his hands.

She also told me that Dr. Bauguess had quit doctoring because he had completely lost his eyesight. Of course, that meant Will lost his job driving the doctor out on house calls, but she added that Will had secured another job with the Civilian Conservation Corp, or C.C.C. for short. He would be leaving soon to work on the Appalachian Scenic Highway.

Bessie verified what my letter said about Daddy, Bertha, and Bonnie Bee moving out to Pound, Virginia so Daddy could work in the Kentucky coal mines. Bessie said they were making the move this coming weekend.

I guess Bertha was happy now that she was rid of all us Elmore kids. My prediction really did come true. Bertha finally talked Daddy into getting rid of us all, and she now has Daddy and Bonnie Bee all to herself.

CHAPTER TWENTY-SEVEN

I did not let Bessie out of my sight when Albert was around. I warned Bessie about Albert without going into too many details, as she was only eleven years old at the time. Bessie might as well have been glued to my side because she went with me everywhere.

I soon started getting behind on my chores because I had Bessie to look after now and she, too, took my time. Aunt Pandy was constantly poking that old bony finger in my face and fussing about my chores not getting done in a timely fashion. I did the best I could do, but now that Bessie was with me she was my first priority; after all, she was all the real family I had left in Wilkes County. Will was up in Virginia working for the C. C. C., Daddy was now working in the Kentucky coal mines, and Bonnie was living in Surry County with the Wilson's. I was sure glad that I did have Bessie because I didn't think I could stand to have everyone living so far away and me being the only one left behind to live in this "God-forsaken" place.

I began to fall behind more and more on my chores, as Bessie and I would often linger outside looking for four leaf clovers, when

Aunt Pandy was not around. By summers end, we had a whole col-
lection of four leaf clovers that were flattened between the pages
of the Bible that Mrs. Cindy, my Sunday school teacher, at the First
United Holiness Church of Jesus Christ gave me. We made special
wishes on every four leaf clover we found before placing them in
the Bible.

I remember a special four leaf clover I found in the field across
the road from the house. The clover was almost the size of a half
dollar, and I knew it was big enough for a whole lot of wishing. I
closed my eyes tight and wished for babies of my own. I wished for
my prince to come and carry me away, giving me enough babies
to fill an entire castle. I placed that clover over Psalm 127 in my
Bible. That Psalm was one of my favorites, and I especially loved
verse three and had even memorized it: *"Lo, children are an heritage
of the Lord: and the fruit of the womb is his reward."*

I knew that more than anything else I wanted to be a momma.
I didn't want to be like Bertha or Aunt Pandy, but I wanted to be
just like my momma, who had love seeping out of every pore in her
body until the Good Lord came and carried her away.

CHAPTER TWENTY-EIGHT

In late fall of 1935, Bessie developed a sore in the bend of her arm. The sore began festering and would weep at night, producing a crust that would cause her arm to stick together at the bend. She would often cry in the morning because her arm would be stuck, and it was painful to straighten. I spent more of my time doctoring Bessie's sore and even less time tending to my chores. Aunt Pandy was not at all concerned about Bessie's arm but was very concerned about my chores being left undone.

One Monday morning after Bessie and my three cousins left for school, instead of doing the wash, I went to search for goldenrod. Before Momma took sick, I had watched her make a poultice with goldenrod flowers to treat a sore that was on Will's leg. She made the poultice daily for about a week, and Will's leg did get better. I figured the same thing would work for Bessie's arm.

I searched half the morning for the goldenrod flowers and, about the time I found some still blooming, Aunt Pandy found me. She walked right over to me and took my face in her rough, old hand and held it up so my eyes were looking right into hers. She growled, "Since your sister got here, you have not been much good around the house. I want you to know, Miss Lucy, that your Uncle Albert and I agreed to let you live here when nobody else would. The agreement we made with your daddy was that you would help out with chores in exchange for your room and board, and you are not keeping up on your end. Now, if you don't get to your chores, I am going to send word to your daddy to come and get you."

I really didn't care if she did send word to Daddy because I was going to look after Bessie's arm whether she liked it or not.

That following Sunday morning, we all piled in Albert's car to go to church. I had spent the morning dressing Bessie's sore, and Aunt Pandy and Albert were not happy with me. When Albert attempted to start the car, it was obvious that the battery was dead. Albert looked up at me in his rearview mirror, "Lucy, you haven't earned your keep lately so you get out and push us down the road until I can roll start this car."

I got out and walked around to the back of his 1932 Ford V8. Using all 90 pounds of my body weight, I began to try to push that car down the driveway. I could see the back of Albert's fat head, with its hair slicked down with oil, and Aunt Pandy's "Sunday go to meeting" hat sitting on top of her long, skinny neck, along with all three of my cousins sitting in the back seat with their faces turned toward me. I got tickled thinking about how this must look. Here was big, fat Albert, Aunt Pandy, Estelle, Agnes, Ennis, and Bessie all sitting in the car, while little ole me was trying to push all of them and the heavy car, too. The harder I tried to push that car the funnier it became and the louder I laughed. Albert and Aunt Pandy must have heard me laughing because Aunt Pandy jumped out of the car and came straight back to where I stood. While firmly placing her hands on her hips she said, "You should be ashamed, Lucy. You are worthless! I am writing your daddy this very evening and telling him to come after you and Bessie because I am fed up with you both. Let's hear you laugh about that!"

I didn't know how to respond to Aunt Pandy; after all, I could not care less if she did write Daddy, but at the same time I knew Bertha would be the one deciding my fate. I responded with a simple, "I'm sorry."

Albert, my cousins, and Bessie got out of the car, and we all made our way back inside. We did not make it to church, but Albert still made us all assemble in the sitting room where he opened his Bible to II Thessalonians, Chapter 3, verse 10 and read these words: "*If any would not work, neither should he eat.*"

He then began his sermon, preaching to the top of his lungs for nearly one hour. During his entire rant, he kept his eyes fixed on me. My three cousins seemed nervous and uncomfortable because they squirmed the entire time that Albert hollered at me. After Albert's long tirade, he excused us all to go to our rooms.

I saw Aunt Pandy picking up her pen and paper as Bessie and I walked to our room. I knew she was fixing to write Daddy. I just prayed that Daddy would make Bertha see that he needed us as much as she needed Bonnie Bee.

CHAPTER TWENTY-NINE

The following morning, after Albert left for work and my cousins and Bessie left for school, I watched Aunt Pandy place a letter into the mailbox and raise the flag. I knew whose address was on that letter, but I just had to see for myself. As soon as Aunt Pandy went back into the house, I walked out to the mailbox and peeked inside. Sure enough the letter was addressed to Daddy. I wasn't upset in the least. I was missing Daddy, and I was ready to move out to Virginia to be with him.

I wondered what Virginia would be like. I remembered Momma's stories about me being born in Virginia, but all my memories were in North Carolina, as I had lived here since I was a year old. I wondered if going back would conjure up some of those forgotten memories of Momma. I could not wait for Bessie to get home from school so I could tell her the news.

When Bessie did arrive home from school, I took her to the field across the road to tell her my secret. I told her that we needed to find a special four leaf clover and make a wish that we would all be together again and live happily ever after. We searched and searched for a clover but could not find a single one, three-leaf or otherwise. I figured the big frost the Friday before must have frozen them all out. I was heartsick because I knew a four leaf clover wished on and pressed between the pages of my Bible would bring us the luck we needed.

That night, after Bessie and I got into bed, I took hold of her hand and told her we needed to pray a special prayer that Daddy would be happy to get that letter and would realize that he needed Bessie, Bonnie and me. We prayed that he would come soon and take us all back to Virginia where we could once again be a family and live happily ever after.

CHAPTER THIRTY

The following Saturday afternoon, I had just walked out to sweep the front porch when I heard a car coming up the gravel road. My heart began pounding out of my chest, and I hollered for Bessie. She came out on the porch and started jumping up and down, as if that would help her see over the hill to the approaching car. It seemed like forever before that car crested the hill, and I could see it was Daddy. I could feel the tears welling up in my eyes. Bessie and I took off running to the car. Before Daddy could even get it into park, I opened his door, and we hugged him tight. When we pulled away from Daddy, he smiled while telling us to gather our things quickly. He explained that we needed to get on the road, as it would be dark before we got back home. Those words, "back home," were music to my ears.

I ran back into the house and gathered my belongings, stuffing them into a paper bag. I helped Bessie with her things, and we rushed back out to Daddy's waiting car. Daddy was standing out in the yard talking to Aunt Pandy and Albert.

Estelle, Agnes, and Ennis, who were playing close by, walked over to tell us goodbye. Estelle reached out to hug me while whispering in my ear, "I still want you to teach me how to cook."

I whispered back, "Maybe one day," but I knew I never wanted to come back here.

Aunt Pandy would not even look at me as I opened the car door. Neither she nor Albert told Bessie or me bye. I hopped into the car, and Bessie got in beside me, and we waited for Daddy to wind up his talking.

I was never as happy as I was when Daddy pulled out of the driveway, and we had the car pointed toward Virginia. On our way home, I told Daddy that he could not have come when I needed him worse; after all, Thanksgiving was this coming Thursday, and we could all be together. I told him that I would cook us all a big Thanksgiving dinner, and maybe we could send for Bonnie and Will to come, too. I rattled on and on about how much better everything would be, and Daddy interjected an occasional, "Um hum."

When we reached the house in Pound, Virginia, I was excited because I knew I was soon to be in my new home. Even though I had never been here, and it was all so unfamiliar, I was with Daddy and Bessie, and that was home enough for me. It was even nice to see Bertha and Bonnie Bee. Bertha hugged Bessie and me, even telling us that she was glad we were here. I just knew that Daddy had finally made Bertha see that we all needed to be together.

That night I went to bed the happiest I had been in ever so long. I knew Bertha was coming around, and tomorrow I would talk her into bringing Bonnie home so we could all be together for Thanksgiving. I drifted off to sleep just knowing that this was going to be the very best Thanksgiving ever.

CHAPTER THIRTY-ONE

I awoke early the following morning and decided to surprise everyone with breakfast. I tiptoed into the kitchen and turned on the light. I closed the door behind me so I would not wake anyone before my surprise breakfast was cooked and on the table. I opened each of the cabinets and peeked inside trying to familiarize myself with the location of all the kitchenware and utensils.

A white Kelvinator hummed over in the corner, and I curiously opened the door to reveal the most beautiful bird egg blue interior with all the cold kept items lying on the racks inside. I was in complete awe. I had seen one of these "newfangled" refrigerators from a distance when I stayed with Aunt Pandy and we visited one of the church ladies, but I had never had the chance to peek inside. I was amazed that Daddy and Bertha actually had one of these. I knew Daddy must be making a lot of money in the coal mine to afford the Kelvinator, plus the electricity to run it. I found eggs, bacon, and milk inside the Kelvinator and took them out to use for breakfast.

I fried the bacon and scrambled the eggs in the bacon grease. I was placing the plates on the table when I heard Daddy cough outside the kitchen door. He opened the door and peeked inside. I smiled my happy smile and told him that I was cooking a surprise breakfast. He forced a grin as he entered the kitchen and closed the door behind him. Daddy took a seat at the table and told me to come over and sit down. He was wringing his hands and clearing his throat as I made my way to the table, and my heart sank. I knew before he opened his mouth that Bertha had talked him into making other arrangements for me and inside I began to panic. Everything seemed to be moving in slow motion as I took my seat beside Daddy.

Daddy put his hand on my shoulder and looked at me ever so long before he opened his mouth, then in a low, sad voice came these words, "Lucy, Bertha and I have found you a place to stay across the Kentucky state line in Jenkins. While working in the mines I have become acquainted with Maynard Painter. He, too, works in the mines, and his wife, Hazel, needs help tending to her children. I know how much you like babies and what good help you are, and I told Maynard that I had the perfect fit. Now, before you go and get all emotional, Bertha and I won't be far behind because we are making the move to Jenkins in the next few weeks, and we will be living in the same holler...... And the good news, Lucy, is that the Painters are willing to pay you two dollars per week."

I could not wrap my mind around all this, and I could not believe that Daddy was sending me away again. I thought to myself, if Aunt Pandy and Albert, my kinfolk could work me so hard and abuse me, all the while never paying me one red cent, what more could happen at the hands of perfect strangers who were willing to pay me two dollars per week?

I could not help but get emotional as the tears began to stream down my cheeks. I pleaded with Daddy to let me stay since the house was bigger, and I would work extra, extra hard and do the whole families' bidding, if he just would not send me to the Painters. Daddy placed a firm hand on my shoulder and said, "Lucy, my mind is made up, and you must go live with the Painters. Two dollars per week is mighty good pay for a girl your age."

He then added, "The Painters want you to come this afternoon, after church, so you can get acquainted before you start work in the morning."

I did not say another word; I just wiped my eyes and got breakfast on the table.

Later that same morning, we all piled into Daddy's car to go to church. I did not hear a word the preacher said because all I could think about was being made to leave home again. When the preacher gave the altar call, I made a beeline to the mourners' bench. My heart was breaking, and I knew Jesus was the only one to fix it. I made a plea to God to help Daddy see that I needed to be with my family and to give him a change of heart, but at the very least to keep Jesus shining in my heart, wherever that might be, and if I was destined to live and work for the Painters, I prayed that God would protect me from all harm.

CHAPTER THIRTY-TWO

That afternoon Daddy and I got into his car. Before he turned the key in the ignition, I asked him if I could spend just one more night with the family so I could have time to prepare myself for this move. I promised him that I would go to the Painters first thing in the morning without any fuss. Daddy's response was a simple, "No."

I watched as he turned the key in the ignition. I prayed that the car would not start, but it fired right up and we were on our way.

It was a quiet ride to the Painters, as I never opened my mouth. I spent the time imagining what this adventure would be like. I pictured Mr. Painter to be somewhat fat with fiery red hair and freckles and Mrs. Painter as pleasantly plump with coal black hair and a sassy attitude. I imagined myself as their slave, only ten times worse than my experience at Aunt Pandy and Albert's; after all, they were going to pay me two dollars per week which was entitlement enough for them to treat me any old way they wished.

When we reached the Kentucky state line my heart started racing. I knew it was not that many miles back to Pound, Virginia where Daddy and Bessie were living for the time being, but to me that was a whole state away. I felt the same pang in my heart I felt when I was in North Carolina and Daddy sent the letter that he was moving to Virginia, but at the same time sending Bessie to live with me. The only difference was that this time he wasn't sending Bessie with me; I was going it alone.

Daddy slowed the car and I watched as he turned into Wright's Holler. It was a steep, narrow road that led right up the side of the mountain. He drove about half-way up the hill and pulled into the drive. The house was nothing like I imagined. There was a porch that ran the full length of the house front with pretty fall flowers planted on either side of the steps. There were no chickens pecking around in the yard, but rather a calico cat that lay sprawled out on the porch swing.

I gathered my things and walked toward the front door with Daddy leading the way. Daddy knocked on the door while I made my way over to pet the cat. The cat opened one eye to slowly shut it again as she began motoring a soft purr. The feel of the soft cat fur and the soothing sounds of the purrs just seemed to calm my nerves.

I heard footsteps inside making their way to the door, and I walked over to stand beside Daddy. I intended to use my very best manners and to be as polite as possible because it was important to me that the Painters like me.

When Mrs. Painter answered the door, she looked nothing like I had her pictured in my mind. She was just a little taller than me and very trim. She had a very pleasant face and brown hair that was rolled tight into a bun that sat on the top of her head. She had very soft features that in some way reminded me of Momma. She smiled and told us to come in.

We all three walked into the sitting room where Mr. Painter sat smoking a pipe and reading the newspaper. He, too, was nothing like I imagined. He was a tall, lanky man with brown hair and a neatly trimmed brown speckled beard. Daddy introduced me to Hazel and Maynard. Using my best manners, I curtsied and graciously stuck out my hand, but Hazel said, "In this house we don't shake hands," and instead she reached over and hugged me tight.

The ice was broken, and I felt I could now breathe a sigh of relief.

After Daddy left, Hazel took me to my room. She told me she had fixed it up just for me. It was so different from my room at Aunt Pandy's. This room was big and bright, with a pink chenille spread on the bed, and the prettiest picture hanging above it of a little girl and boy crossing a broken bridge with an angel hovering over them. Instead of a foot locker, I had my own closet, along with a dresser and nightstand.

Hazel told me to put my things away and get settled, and I could then meet her back downstairs for some cookies and milk. Cookies and milk.....COOKIES AND MILK! It had been ever so long since I had cookies and milk. I thought maybe I had died and gone to heaven. I put my things away and tiptoed back downstairs to where Hazel was waiting. She led me into the kitchen, and we sat down at the table where I ate two huge sugar cookies and drank a large glass of ice cold milk.

Hazel talked to me while I ate. I mean, she talked to me, like I was a real human being with real human feelings. She asked questions about me and really seemed to want to get to know who I was. I guess we had been talking about an hour when I heard a baby cry. Hazel said, "That's Joshua. I'll be right back."

In no time Hazel came back into the room carrying the cutest little boy with curly, blonde hair and the bluest eyes. She said, "Joshua, this is Lucy, and you are really going to like this sweet, pretty lady."

She then looked at me and said, "Lucy, meet Joshua. He is your typical, stubborn two- year old."

She sat Joshua in his high chair and had just given him a bottle of milk and a broken cookie when I heard another baby cry. She left the room and a couple of minutes later she came back carrying a true baby in her arms. Hazel walked over to where I was sitting and said, "Lucy, this is Ella."

I responded with, "She is beautiful. How old is she?"

"Six months," was the response.

I asked, "Can I hold her?"

Hazel placed her in my arms, and it took me back to the first time Momma let me hold Bessie. I thought Ella was the second prettiest baby ever born, and I knew right then I wanted to be a momma more than anything else in the whole wide world. I could not help myself; I began to hum and sang my song to Baby Ella, changing my name to hers. Hazel looked at me with tender eyes and asked where I had heard that beautiful song. I replied, "It's really my song because my momma made up the song for me the day I was born and sung it to me until the day she died."

Hazel smiled, "I know your momma was very special, and you are very fortunate to have had a momma like that."

Then I heard her say the sweetest words, "Lucy, you, too, are a very special young lady, and I know God has big plans for you."

I smiled back at Hazel, and I thought to myself, I am really going to like living here.

CHAPTER THIRTY-THREE

I slept soundly in my new bed and woke up completely refreshed. I peeked out the window to a late fall sun peeking through the bare trees over the hilltop.

I went to the closet and pulled out my best hand- me -down dress, the one made of a pink flour sack with white rick rack lace covering the hemline. I wanted to look as special to Hazel as she thought me to be. I combed through my long, blonde hair and tried to place it in a tight bun on top of my head like Hazel had worn yesterday, but I could not get my hair to cooperate the way hers had.

I tiptoed downstairs and found Hazel in the sitting room rocking Ella. She smiled and asked how I slept.

I replied, "Like a rock."

I asked if she wanted me to start breakfast. She told me that she had already sent Maynard off to work, and I need not worry about breakfast for anyone but myself. She took Ella back to her room and placed her in the crib. She then joined me in the kitchen. She showed me around and told me that I was allowed to cook and eat anything I wanted. I caught a glimpse of the cornmeal up in the cabinet and decided a cornbread cake was just perfect for this occasion. I watched the batter float around in the grease like I always did and daydreamed about Momma. I knew my momma would be happy for me to be living here, and I just knew if she was still alive she, too, would love Hazel just as much as I was beginning to love her.

CHAPTER THIRTY-FOUR

Working for the Painters was much more a blessing and less a curse. Hazel and Maynard treated me like family instead of a hired hand. Granted, they did pay me my two dollars a week, of which one dollar had to go back home to Daddy. (I knew that was at Bertha's insistence.) I would work extra hard scrubbing the floors and cleaning the house because I loved the Painters. I wanted to please them because they were so good to me.

In a short time, I fell in love with Joshua and Ella and enjoyed more than anything else getting to tend to them. I just knew that God's big plan for me was to one day give me young'uns of my own.

One evening before bed, I was talking to Hazel and asked her about the possibility of me returning to school. I told her how much I had loved school and was only two months shy of completing the eighth grade. I asked if she had any concerns with me finishing school. Hazel's eyes lit up, and she told me she thought that going back to school was a great idea, but that decision must be left up to my daddy.

I waited until Christmas before I talked to Daddy about going back to school. By this time, he and Bertha had also moved to Wright's Holler and were living a little further up the hill. I walked up to the house to spend Christmas day with Daddy and Bessie, and I caught Daddy alone out on the porch gathering wood for the stove. I told him of my desire to return to school while he gathered the wood, but all I could get out of him was a few grunts. Finally, I just came right out and asked, "Daddy, would it be ok for me to go to school in Jenkins?"

He looked at me for a minute and then said, "Lucy, I think you first need to save your money and buy you some proper school clothes, and then we might talk about it."

I thought, well, at least, he didn't tell me "No." Who knows, God's special plan for me may be to grow up, and not only have babies of my own, but to be a teacher or maybe a nurse.

That evening I could not wait to tell Hazel. I told Hazel what Daddy had said about saving my money to buy some school clothes. Hazel said, "Lucy, I have an idea. You can save your money, and we can buy some material and make you some clothes. That will be cheaper, and it should not take you long to save that much money. In fact, you may be able to finish the eighth grade before this school year is over."

I ran up to my room and pulled my money box out of the nightstand. I counted out a whole sixty-seven cents! I decided no more Coca-Colas or Mars bars from Johnson's store until I had my school clothes.

CHAPTER THIRTY-FIVE

Beside the fact that I got to live with the Painter's, living in Wright's Holler also had other advantages. There were lots of neighbors, many of whom were B-O-Y-S. I was just about to turn sixteen, and I was beginning to take notice of the opposite sex. There was one particular boy that lived at the top of the hill named Randall Mackswell, and he made my heart flutter. He was very clean cut with curly, brown hair that tousled about in the wind and the nicest dimples in both cheeks. I found out from Bonnie Bee that he was seventeen and on the football team at Jenkins Independent School. Every time I was out on the porch when he passed, he would always smile and wave at me. This would cause my heart to almost pound out of my chest.

One day in early spring he passed while I was out sweeping the steps. To my amazement, he stopped and asked me what I thought about the nice weather we were having. I could not think of a single intelligent thing to say, and I opened my mouth and out came the response, "I think it's really cute."

He gave me a puzzled look, "Huh?"

"I meant nice; I think it is really nice. Yes, spring is a nice, cute time of the year."

He shrugged, "If you say so," and walked on down the hill.

I slapped my forehead with the palm of my hand, while replaying my dumb remarks in my mind. What a stupid thing to say; I knew that I just ruined my chances with the cutest boy in town.

I could not believe it when Randall sent word by Bessie the following week that he would like to court me. Bertha, too, got wind of this because she marched down to the Painters later the same afternoon and forbade me from seeing Randall Mackswell; after all, her Bonnie Bee had took notice of him, too.

I did not say a word to Bertha about my crush on Randall, but after she left, Hazel looked at me and said, "Lucy, date who you want to, but be careful who you marry. Bertha might be tough, but she can't slide down barbed wire."

I wrinkled up my nose and laughed at Hazel's comment. I wasn't really sure what she meant, but I knew if I was going to court Randall Mackswell it was going to be behind Bertha's back.

I did sneak around and court Randall Mackswell a few times. We would innocently sit in the Painter's sitting room and talk about the weather and football- one of the many sports I knew nothing about. To be honest, it became a little boring.

It was on the fourth date that I realized Randall was not my Prince Charming. He was getting ready to leave and leaned in to give me my first ever real kiss. It was nothing like I expected. I did not see fireworks, and my heart did not catch on fire; I merely felt sick. I pulled away quickly, wiped my entire mouth on my sleeve, and showed him to the door. I'm sure he did not enjoy the kiss any more than I did because that was the last time Randall Mackswell ever came calling on me.

CHAPTER THIRTY-SIX

I finally saved enough money to buy me some material for my new school clothes and just in time for my sixteenth birthday. As a special birthday present The Painter's drove me to Whitesburg, and Hazel helped me pick out the patterns and fabric at Buttons and Bows Fabric Shop. I was so excited with my selections and could not wait for Daddy to see that I now would have proper school clothes.

Hazel was a great seamstress and taught me the basics of sewing. I helped to cut out the patterns, but it was Hazel who actually sewed my dresses, as I did not want to risk messing them up. When we were finished, I had four new dresses that were proper; not only for school, but for the Queen's tea should I be invited. I could not wait to show off my new dresses for Daddy.

That following Sunday I wore one of my new dresses to church, and after the service I waited outside for Daddy. I wanted him to notice that I now had proper school clothes. When he emerged from the church, I ran over and twirled around while saying, "Well, what do you think?"

Daddy responded, "Is that a new dress?"

"Yes, and I have three more just as pretty...so now can I go back to school?"

Daddy frowned, "Not now, Lucy, but maybe some time."

I could feel the tears coming and I did not want Daddy or anyone else to see me cry, so I turned and walked to the Painters car where the entire Painter family sat waiting. Hazel sensed that I was upset, and she just handed me a tissue out of her pocketbook. She knew me almost as well as my momma did, so she did not press me for details; she just let me be until I was ready to talk.

Later that evening, Hazel asked me to come out and sit in the porch swing with her for a spell. I walked out and took my seat beside her, as she handed me a glass of tea. We sat rocking the longest time while I silently sipped my ice tea. All at once, I began to talk. It was like I opened my mouth, and those words just spilled out without my ability to stop them. I told her how upset and hurt I was that Daddy would not let me go to school, and now I would never get to be a nurse or a teacher, and I just felt like giving up. I bared my soul to Hazel and told her my thoughts and feelings that I had never been able to share with anyone else. She never opened her mouth; rather she listened until I was emptied of all my words.

She then took me by the hand and said, "Lucy, I know you are hurt and upset, and you have every right to be, but I want you to know that the only thing finishing school can get you that you don't already have is a diploma."

She looked me dead in the eyes and said, "Lucy, you are just as smart as anyone I have ever known. Why, you have something that the other students at Jenkins Independent School do not have. You have been afforded an Ester Elmore raising, and that has made you wise beyond your years. You always hold your head high because you hold inside you something that is very special, and I knew that the first time I met you."

I smiled at Hazel and hugged her tight. It was almost like she could see inside my heart, and I loved her all the more for truly caring about me. That night, when I crawled into bed, I thanked God for Hazel Painter because she was the one who was helping me to keep my bright light shining.

CHAPTER THIRTY-SEVEN

I did not give going to school much thought after that day. It was not that I did not want to go, but I knew that whether I went to school or not, it was not going to affect my ability to have babies, and having babies was what I wanted most out of life, anyway.

I spent the next school year tending to Joshua and Ella, all the while daydreaming about what my family would look like some day. I wondered who I would marry, where we might live, and how many children I would have. I knew I wanted a whole houseful of kids. I wanted to have so many that I could be called, "kid poor," as my momma would say.

One sunny, Saturday afternoon, I was sitting out on the porch swing watching Joshua push his cars across the porch when I caught a glimpse of a man walking from Wright's Holler over to Brickyard Hill. I had never seen him before, but he sure caught my eye. He had manly good looks, was dapperly dressed, and walked with a confident gait. I thought to myself, now that's my idea of Prince Charming, and if he ever comes back riding a white horse, I will wave my handkerchief in the air and maybe he will rescue this damsel in distress. I laughed out loud at the thought. Joshua looked up at me and began laughing, too.

I picked Joshua up and took him inside. I walked into the kitchen where Hazel was peeling apples to make a pie. I asked her if someone had moved into Old Ren's boarding house. She said that a gentleman from Wise, Virginia had just started working with Maynard in the coal mines, and he was moving into the boarding house.

I asked, "Do you know his name?"

Hazel replied, "I think they call him Whitey."

I thought to myself, Whitey? He looks much too sophisticated to have a name like that.

I coyly asked, "Is he married?"

Hazel looked at me suspiciously and said, "I don't know, but I don't think so. Why do you ask, Miss Lucy? Are you interested?"

I knew my face was getting flushed so I turned toward the door and said, "Oh no! I just think it neighborly to know all you can about those living around you."

I could feel Hazel looking at me, and I turned back around to smile. She winked at me and said, "I don't remember you asking any neighborly questions when Clarence and Gertie moved up on the hill."

I did not have a retort, so I just turned and walked back into the sitting room to look after Joshua.

The next evening, as I was taking the dirty dishwater out to sling on the flowers by the porch, Whitey came walking down the hill. He caught glimpse of me and tipped his hat. I held my hand about waist high and waved my fingers back at him. He smiled a broad smile at me as he passed by on his way over to Brickyard Hill. I whispered, "I think My Prince has finally arrived."

I went to bed that night swooning at the thought of Whitey. We had not even spoken to each other, yet I knew he was the one for me. I intended to find out as much as I could about my new neighbor. I could not wait until morning because I knew just the person that could help me, while keeping my secret under wraps.

CHAPTER THIRTY-EIGHT

The next morning I waited outside on the porch for Bessie to walk by on her way to school. I told her about the charming man that had moved into Old Ren's Boarding House. I knew Bessie could get information about Whitey without seeming suspicious because she often visited Old Ren after school. I made her pinky promise not to spill the beans on me because I did not want anyone knowing about my crush on Whitey, especially not Bertha or Bonnie Bee. Bessie loved secret missions as she called them, and she promised to come back with classified information on Whitey.

I was outside at the clothesline beating the rugs when I heard Bessie whistling as she made her way across the hill. She caught a glimpse of me at the clothesline and came running. She smiled at me and teasingly asked, "How much is my newfound information on Whitey worth to you?"

She then paused and said, "Is it worth...say....a Mars Bar?"

Bessie knew that I loved Mars Bars and kept a small stash in my nightstand. I responded, "It is definitely worth a Mars Bar if you tell me everything, and don't leave out a single, sordid detail."

She grinned great big and said, "Deal!"

I quietly made my way up to my room to get the Mars Bar. My heart was pounding inside my chest, and I felt giddy all over, but I did not want to raise Hazel's suspicions because I wasn't ready to reveal that I indeed had a crush on Whitey, at least not yet. I put the Mars Bar in my apron pocket and made my way back out to where Bessie sat waiting on the porch swing. I handed her the Mars Bar, and she started to rip open the wrapper, but I stopped her and said, "No eating until you give me every single crumb of information you have."

She began fidgeting with the hem line on her dress and said, "Give me just a minute to remember it all."

She closed her eyes and cleared her throat, and when her eyes reopened so did her mouth and all that "classified information" just poured out like a river. After Bessie finished spitting out all that good juicy information, I knew that Whitey's real name was Alexander Hornaday, and he was definitely in his twenties. I thought, Alexander Hornaday, what a sophisticated name for a sophisticated man. He truly was a man and not a mere boy like that Randall Mackswell.

Bessie went on to tell me that he moved here from Wise, Virginia because Consolidated Coal Company had hired him as their main coal cutter. Old Ren told her that word had it he was considered the very best coal cutter in the Eastern Appalachian region. Old Ren also told Bessie that Alexander had paid his room and board a full month in advance, so it looked like he would be staying around here long enough for me to get up my nerve to at least speak to him. I asked Bessie if she had found out if he was spoken for, to which Bessie replied, "Old Ren didn't say anything about that, but I'll try to get that information tomorrow if you are willing to let go of another Mars Bar."

I told Bessie if she could produce that information I could definitely part with another Mars Bar.

The following afternoon, Bessie showed up at the front door, and I already had her Mars Bar in my apron pocket. She informed me that Old Ren did not know anything about Alexander's personal affairs. Thinking Bessie must be the one interested, she chastened her that he was much too old for her anyway. Bessie promised that she had kept this covert operation under wraps and just let Old Ren continue to believe that it was she who was interested.

CHAPTER THIRTY-NINE

The following Friday night I decided to treat Bessie to a hot dog and movie at the Recreation Building (the hub of social activity in Jenkins). <u>Carefree,</u> the new movie starring Ginger Rogers and Fred Astaire, was playing. I sorely wanted to see this movie because I loved Ginger Rogers and secretly wanted to look and dance like her. I was also hoping for the possibility of seeing Alexander there.

I decided to wear my bright blue dress, which was my favorite because it brought out the blue in my eyes. I was hoping if Alexander showed up he, too, would take notice. I pulled my hair into a bun on the top of my head just like Hazel's in case he did show up and take notice. I wanted to let him know I had the maturity of a woman and was not a mere girl.

I waited out on the porch for Bessie so we could walk over to the Recreation Building together. Bessie came bouncing down the hill chomping on a huge wad of bubble gum that was obviously too big for her mouth. I told her she needed to spit out about half of that gum wad because it made her lips look funny. She spit the whole wad into the drain ditch and wiped her mouth on her arm. She looked at me with puckered lips and said, "Now, is that better?"

I gave her a wink and a smile as we made our way over to the Recreation Building.

I informed Bessie since I was the one paying for the hot dog and movie that she must take on an undercover mission. She smiled and, while excitedly rolling her hands around in front of her face, squealed, "Oh boy! What is it?"

I told her that she must be on the lookout for Alexander, and if she spied him to nonchalantly let me know.

We walked into the café and ordered two hot dogs with chili and slaw and made our way over to a booth to sit down. We had not even taken our first bite when Bessie started rubbing my arm like she was about to take the hide off, while announcing in a very loud whisper, "I see him! I see him! He just walked into the door!"

My heart started racing, and I could feel my face getting flushed, but I managed to admonish Bessie once again, reminding her that this was an undercover mission.

In a few short minutes, Alexander took a seat in the next booth over, with a hot dog on his tray. He was dressed to the nines with his coal black hair slicked back with tonic, and he looked like an absolute dream. I noticed that he did not have anyone with him, so I could now assume that he was not taken.

I could feel all the butterflies gathering in my stomach, and I did not think I could swallow the bite of hot dog I had swirling around in my mouth. I knew I could never eat the whole hot dog, so I cut it in half and asked Bessie if she would like the untouched half. She quickly swiped it from my plate and had eaten hers and mine before I could force what little hot dog that remained on my plate down my throat.

The whole time we sat there my eyes wanted to stay fixed on Alexander, but I did not want to appear overly interested. I wondered if he had noticed me because I had not seen him look my way, and my eyes had been darting in his direction every half a second. As I put that last bite of hot dog in my mouth, Bessie picked up her drink and quickly gulped down what remained. "Come on, Lucy; let's get on into the theater so we can get good seats."

I glared at her, "Can you, please, just hold your horses?"

I watched as Alexander stood and walked over to the ticket counter to purchase his movie ticket, then I said, "Come on, Bessie; let's get our tickets."

We walked over and stood right behind Alexander as he was being handed his ticket. As he turned to make his way into the theater, our eyes met. He nodded his head and said, "It's a pleasure to see you again."

I was determined I wasn't going to say anything stupid like I did when I met Randall. I smiled and said, "The pleasure is all mine."

I could not believe those words just came out of my mouth. I thought to myself, that was worse than saying something stupid. Now he probably thinks that I am some swooning floosy. He smiled a broad smile at me, exposing his pearly white teeth, and said, "Can I pay for your ticket?" I smiled back and looked down at my feet to try to appear coy, "I guess that would be ok."

After purchasing the tickets, he looked at me and said, "And what's the name of the pretty young lady I just had the pleasure of buying a movie ticket?"

I responded, "Lucy...Lucy Elmore."

He reached out his hand to shake mine. "Lucy Elmore, I'm Alexander Hornaday, but everyone calls me Whitey, and it's very nice to meet you."

He then turned and stuck out his arm and said, "May I have the pleasure of ushering you in to see this picture show."

I took his arm and smiled, "Most certainly."

As we walked arm in arm into the theater I felt dizzy and flush, and my hands were sweating something fierce. I thought I might just be dreaming, so I reached over and pinched my arm just to make sure this was real. He sat down next to me with Bessie at my other side.

As sorely as I had wanted to see the movie, I could not tell you a single thing that happened because my mind was running crazy and spinning all around the entire time we sat there. After the movie was over, Alexander looked over at me and said, "Miss Lucy, could I have the pleasure of walking you home?"

I smiled up at him and said, "The pleasure would be mine."

We both laughed as he stuck out his arm for me to take hold.

Bessie ran ahead of us all the way home, and we lingered back. Alexander asked how I liked the movie, to which I responded, "I just love Ginger Rogers."

Alexander said, "Well, I think you and she look a lot alike."

I said, "You really think so?"

He responded, "Definitely!"

He could not have given me a greater compliment. As we walked up onto the Painter's porch Alexander said, "Lucy, would it be ok if I come calling on you again?"

I put my hand up to my forehead to push back a strand of hair that had fallen down around my eyes, "I would really like that."

Alexander took hold of my hand, and with his index finger and thumb, he placed the strand of hair behind my ear. He then took that same index finger and, while pushing my chin up, leaned down and kissed my cheek. I felt this crazy tingle all over my body, and I thought to myself, now that's a real kiss! My Prince is finally here!

CHAPTER FORTY

Alexander came calling every night the following week. He would get to the house about seven every evening, and we would sit out on the porch swing, drink sweet tea, and talk. He was so interesting and easy to talk to that I felt like I had known him my whole life.

Alexander told me about his work in the coal mines. His daddy introduced him to the mines when he was only eight years old. He told me he remembered going to the coal mine with his Uncle Hank who was applying for a job, and it was around the same time his Daddy's shift was exiting the mine. "My daddy appeared from that dark mine all black and dusty, and he saw me standing outside waiting for Hank. Daddy asked me if I would like to take a short ride back into the mine and, of course, I did. I remember he took off his carbide helmet and placed it on my head. It all but covered my whole face, and then we got into that coal car and headed off into the belly of that mine. I loved the damp, earthy smell and how much cooler it felt inside the mine on that hot, summer day, and I got bit by the mining fever. The day I turned fifteen I went to work for Southeastern Coal Corporation, and I have worked the mines ever since," recounted Alexander.

I told him that I heard he was the best coal cutter in the Eastern Appalachians.

He blushed, "Well, I don't know about that, but coal mining is definitely in my blood, and I guess I will mine until the day I die."

He also informed me that he was twenty-nine years old and asked how I felt about him being so much older. I told him that I was ok with that because I thought of myself as a very mature seventeen year old.

I asked him how he got the nickname Whitey. Alexander explained that after a long day in the mine the only parts of his body showing that were not covered in black coal dust were the whites of his eyes and his teeth. Since he was always smiling, with his pearly whites exposed, he got stamped with the nickname Whitey, which stuck.

I told him that I preferred to call him Alexander. He smiled a crooked smile and said, "Lucy, you can call me anything you wish."

Alexander wanted to know how I came to live with the Painters since my parents were living in the same holler.

I told him my whole life story from the time my momma died until I came to live here. He looked at me after I finished and said, "Well, I guess you are a very mature seventeen year old, Lucy Elmore."

He then tenderly looked into my eyes, and while brushing the back of his hand across my forehead said, "I knew from the first time I saw you that there was something special about you, and I know now what it is, Miss Lucy."

He did not say anything else but just continued smiling his crooked smile, all the while rubbing my forehead and gazing into my eyes.

I finally said, "Well, don't leave me hanging! What it is?"

With his gaze fixed on me like he was peering deep into my soul he said, "Lucy, you do have a way of stealing a man's heart."

I smiled as he gently lifted my chin and said, "May I kiss you, Lucy Elmore?"

I closed my eyes and whispered, "The pleasure would be all mine."

When his lips touched mine, it was like lightning bolts were surging through my entire body, and I knew at that moment he, too, had stolen my heart, and this was the man that I would one day marry.

CHAPTER FORTY-ONE

I was ready to let the world know that I had the biggest crush on Alexander Hornaday, so I decided to invite him to Daddy and Bertha's. Even though Daddy already knew Alexander from working in the mines, I was ready for him to know that I was smitten with Alexander, and I so wanted his approval. I asked Alexander if he would like to go up and officially meet my family.

He looked at me with concern in his eyes. "Lucy, before I officially meet your family there is something you need to know about me that may change your mind."

I thought to myself, "Nothing could ever change my mind about you. I couldn't care less if you sprouted three heads, I would still be just as crazy about you."

He rubbed his furrowed brow as he began to speak, "Lucy, I'm divorced, and I have two children, Chloe, who is eleven, and James, who is eight."

I could feel the blood draining out of my face and everything started spinning around, so I just sat right down on the porch step.

He sat down next to me, "I have wanted to tell you this, but I just could not find the words."

I opened my mouth to respond, and I knew how he felt because my words were stuck down deep in my throat. I felt the tears welling up in my eyes so I took a deep breath, cleared my throat, and attempted to swallow the lump that was lodged there. I hesitated for a moment, then looked up into his eyes and said, "Will you tell me exactly what happened?"

He took my hand, "I promise you, Lucy, that it was not my idea. I intended to stay married forever, but Rachel had other plans. By the way, her name was Rachel. We married young, and after James started school Rachel grew restless. We had taken in a boarder named Ben, who happened to be a fellow miner, but their relationship became more than friendly. One day I came home from work to find a note in place of her and the kids. She left me for Ben and took my kids with her. That's the long and short of it."

In a trembling voice, I said, "Do you see your kids?"

He shrugged, "I write to them every week and send money, but rarely get responses. I know Rachel intercepts the letters, and she has tried to make me out as the bad guy. If it's any consolation I have been divorced for almost two years, and I am ready to move on with my life. That is how I ended up in Jenkins."

I began rattling off about Bertha being divorced. I explained how she and her first husband had divided up their children, and how Jasper ended up dying of a broken heart.

He took hold of my hand, "What are you trying to say, Lucy?"

I replied, "I could never leave my kids, if God ever blesses me with any, and I always want them to have me and their daddy."

Alexander hugged me tight and said, "Knowing how you are, Lucy, I would never expect anything less, but I want you to know that it was not my intent to leave my children or wife. I will always try to be there for my children, and I will continue to do what I can for them."

He added, "I know that's a whole lot to take in right now, so before this relationship goes any farther I want to give you a chance to digest all this."

He turned and kissed me on the forehead, and I sat on the porch step watching as he walked back down the road toward Brickyard Hill.

I stood and ran into the house, straight for my room. I flung myself on the bed and buried my head in the pillow, and I began sobbing uncontrollably. I knew that I was falling in love with Alexander, but I needed to sort this all out in my mind. I must have cried myself to sleep because I awoke having dreamed about Momma.

In my dream, Momma and I were back home in Wilkesboro. I was watching Momma fry cornbread cakes while I told her about Alexander. I told her that I was real smitten with him, but I knew we could never be together because he was divorced and had kids of his own.

She patted my hand and said, "Lucy, I know with your big heart you can find enough love inside for Alexander and his children. If you truly love him don't deprive yourself or make him suffer for something that can't be undone or changed. Lucy, I know you will make the right decision; after all, I named you Lucy for a reason."

Momma leaned over and kissed my cheek just as I awoke.

I sat up on my bed and pulled free the hair fastened to my face with tears and, catching a glimpse of myself in the mirror, I smiled because I knew I had gotten Momma's stamp of approval, and that meant more to me than anything.

CHAPTER FORTY-TWO

The following week Alexander was officially meeting my family and just in time for my eighteenth birthday. I must say I was a little nervous as we walked up onto Daddy and Bertha's porch. Bessie saw us and came running out to meet us, all the while squealing, as she ran around behind me to put her hands up over my eyes. She said, "Lucy, I have a big surprise for you!"

When she took her hands away from my eyes there stood Bonnie holding a birthday cake. I knew Bonnie was on her way out to Jenkins to work for the Johnson's who lived on B & O Hill, but I did not think she would be here until the first of August. I could not believe it! I had not seen Bonnie since our house burned down, and she was not the little tomboy that I remembered. Bonnie was now a beautiful young woman. My mouth flew open as I was aghast.

Bonnie giggled, "Seeing me with this cake in my hands rendered you speechless, didn't it? Well, don't worry, Bessie baked the cake, but she wanted me to surprise you with it."

I reached out to hug her, and she lost her grip on the cake, and we watched as the cake slid right off the plate and onto the porch. I laughed and said, "Well, some things never change."

Bonnie rolled her eyes, "I'll have you know that I have learned a thing or two about cooking in the last three years, Lucy, and it looks like your good cooking has done hooked you a man."

I turned to Alexander, "Bonnie, this is Alexander...Alexander Hornaday."

Alexander stuck out his hand as he and Bonnie exchanged pleasantries.

I asked Bessie to get me a broom and dustpan, so we could clean up the cake. Bonnie said, "Not before we stick a candle in it for you to blow out."

I smiled, "You're not serious."

She smiled back, "I am very serious. You know its bad luck if you don't make a wish on your birthday cake and blow out the candle, and it looks to me like you have a whole lot to wish for."

I coyly smiled. "I reckon I do."

Everyone, including Bertha and Bonnie Bee came out on the porch and sang, "Happy Birthday," as I blew out the candle on the "Chocolate -Upside -Down Cake," as Bonnie called it.

After the mess was cleaned up, we all went inside where I officially introduced Alexander as my steady. I was so proud to be Alexander's girl. After all, he was smart and stylish, with the best manners, not to mention all his manly good looks.

Daddy and Alexander hit it off immediately, talking about their work in the mines. I had never heard Daddy talk that much, ever.

We girls went into the kitchen while Daddy and Alexander sat in the sitting room talking. We sat around the table while Bertha rinsed some cherries, placed them in a bowl, and set them in the middle of the table. Before Bertha sat down, she gave me a pat on the back and whispered, "Lucy, you hold onto him; he's a keeper."

I could not have been happier. We girls sat around the table, eating cherries, and talking about everything under the sun.

As the day began to fade into twilight, Daddy asked us girls to come back into the sitting room where he tuned his Delco Radio to the Grand Ole Opry. I took my seat beside Alexander as we all gathered around for the music. As those songs began to flow from the radio, my feet would not keep still. I sat beside Alexander, patting his leg, while my feet kept beat to the music. The Opry Show ended that night with the Bill Monroe song, "Rollin My Sweet Baby's Arms." Alexander reached over and took my hand, squeezing it tight. I felt that tingly feeling all over my body, and I just knew this was right.

Alexander walked me home that evening under a blanket of stars and a waning moon. As we walked onto the porch he asked me to have a seat on the porch swing. I sat down as he stooped over by the steps and pulled a box from underneath. He handed me the box, and I opened it to reveal a beautiful gold watch. He took the watch from my hand and turned it over revealing the engraved words "My time spent with you is more valuable than gold."

Alexander smiled his crooked smile and said, "Happy Birthday, Lucy."

I reached up and hugged him tight. He whispered into my ear, "I love you, Lucy Elmore."

I whispered back, "And I so love you."

He leaned in and kissed me, and when my eyes opened the fireflies seemed to be putting on an extra-special light show just for us.

CHAPTER FORTY-THREE

During the coming months, I could feel myself falling deeper and deeper in love with Alexander. I felt so happy and seemed to have more energy. Hazel had noticed too and said that I had taken on a special glow. I knew that Alexander was the one with whom I wanted to spend the rest of my life. He was my Prince Charming, and wherever we lived I would make it our castle and fill it with lots of babies.

The week before Christmas Alexander told me that he would not be down on Friday night because he needed to go up and talk to my daddy. I thought to myself, I bet he is going to ask Daddy for my hand in marriage. We had recently been talking a lot about marriage. I was ready to marry Alexander but scared at the same time. I was beginning to feel very vulnerable, as Alexander now carried my heart in his hand.

That very night I went to bed, and I dreamed about Bertha and Jasper. I dreamed that Bertha and her husband, Bill, were parting ways. There stood Jasper, wanting both of them and not wanting to leave the only home he had ever known. There was Bertha, tugging on the one side of Jasper, and Bill pulling on the other. I was screaming, "Stop it! You're hurting him!"

Jasper was crying with Bill and Bertha on opposite sides of him screaming, "Let go; he's mine!"

I just knew they were going to pull him in two or, at the very least, pull his arms clean out of socket. I didn't know what to do, so I just began screaming Momma's quote to the top of my lungs, "'*It's a great life if you don't weaken, but who wants to be strong.*'"

I awoke with that quote still on my lips. While brushing my hair, I took a good long look at myself in the mirror. I mouthed to myself, "Now I get it! I really get Momma's quote!"

Having fallen hopelessly in love with Alexander, I knew what the quote meant; at least, what it meant for me at this time in my life. For me, the quote meant that no matter how strong I was I had to let my guard down and be vulnerable to fall in love. In fact, it's the only way to ever truly fall in love. I must now rely on Alexander to stay strong and protect my heart and vice versa.

If Bertha and Bill had lived by this quote, they would not have ended up divorced and Jasper may not have died. I was determined that I was not going to end up divorced. Alexander had placed his heart in the palm of my hand, and I intended to protect it as if it were the finest gold. I could only hope he would do the same for mine.

After I finished with my hair, I powdered my face and put on a little rouge before going downstairs. Hazel was in the kitchen, and I asked her if it would be ok if I went into town for a few minutes.

She asked if Alexander was joining me there.

I told her he was not because I was going to Dalymeyer's Jewelry Store to buy his Christmas present.

She quizzically asked, "What in the world are you going to buy him at the jewelry store?"

I winked, "I'll show you when I get back."

Dalymeyer's had exactly what I was looking for, and I could not wait to get back and show it to Hazel.

Upon my return, Hazel was in the kitchen making homemade fudge. I walked over to the table and carefully took out my jewelry store purchase. I asked Hazel to come over and take a look at the gold heart that was divided into two parts but when placed together formed a complete heart with these words engraved: *"Love is composed of a single soul sharing two bodies. Aristotle"*

I told Hazel about my dream and about Momma's quote- how I had come to figure out what it meant for me. I also told her how serious I was about Alexander and how important and serious marriage was to me.

I explained, "I want him to understand how important it is to me for him to always protect my heart, just as I will protect his."

I told her that I intended to give him half of the heart, and I was going to keep the other half, and as long as we were together our heart would be complete.

She smiled, "Lucy, I know Alexander will love it! You, Lucy, are one very special young lady, but as I've said before, I knew that all along."

As I placed my purchase back into the small box, I smiled back at her, *"'It's a great life if you don't weaken, but who wants to be strong.'"*

CHAPTER FORTY-FOUR

It is Christmas! Glorious Christmas! Santa sure must have thought I was good this year because he sent Prince Charming, who in turn, got down on one knee bearing the sweetest marriage proposal, along with the most beautiful ring. I had dreamed my whole life how this day would be, but it topped my greatest expectations. As I accepted Alexander's marriage proposal, I took his face in my hands, and I kissed him with all the intensity I could muster. I then reached into my apron pocket and took out the present I had for him. He opened the box to reveal half the heart. He had a puzzled look on his face, but I immediately took the other half out of my apron pocket and placed them together to reveal the whole heart with the engraved words. Alexander rubbed his fingers over the words: *"Love is composed of a single soul sharing two bodies. Aristotle"*

"Do you really mean this, Lucy?"

I nodded, "Yes. I just wish I had thought of it before Aristotle did."

We both laughed, and then I cleared my throat. "I want you to know, Alexander Hornaday, that you hold my heart in the palm of your hand, just as I hold yours. Now, I intend to treat yours just as I would the most precious gold, and I would be most grateful if you would treat mine the same. That's the reason for my gift. You see one half you keep and the other half I keep, and as long as we are together, we always have a complete heart."

Alexander lovingly looked at me, "Lucy, I will always treat your heart as if it was hand-blown glass, and I promise, if left in my care, it will never break."

I smiled up at him and hugged him tight.

Later on that evening, I asked Alexander to accompany me up to Daddy and Bertha's because I wanted them to see my ring and also to officially introduce him as my fiancé.

Upon our arrival, Daddy, Bertha, Bonnie, Bessie, and Bonnie Bee were all in the sitting room listening to the radio, drinking egg nog, and eating Christmas cookies. I stuck out my ring finger and said, "I would like for you all to meet my fiancé."

Bonnie and Bessie shrieked, "Oh, Lucy, your ring is so pretty!"

Everyone hugged us and gave us their best wishes.

I went into the kitchen and poured Alexander and myself a cup of egg nog and returned to the sitting room. A song I had never heard before, "I've Got My Love to Keep Me Warm," echoed from Daddy's Delco. I reached up and entwined my arm in Alexander's arm, and we swayed back and forth to the music. We stayed and visited until the radio station signed off for the evening.

The snow and sleet were beginning to blanket the holler as Alexander walked me home that evening and, as cold as the thermometer said the air temperature was, I felt all nice and toasty because the fire in my heart was keeping me warm.

CHAPTER FORTY-FIVE

A lexander and I were getting married! As a young girl I had dreamed of a big church wedding with a virtual flower garden surrounding the altar and every kind of flower imaginable cascading from each of the pews. I imagined myself in a long flowing gown that was all decorated in ribbons and lace.

We decided to waste no time, but to get married right away. I had only managed to save about forty-two dollars while working for the Painters. I knew it would take years to save up enough to have a wedding of the magnitude of which I dreamed, so I decided on a simple wedding at the Seco United Church of God. On January 21, 1939, I became Lucy Hornaday in a simple ceremony with my immediate family present.

We made our first home in a Company house on B & O Hill. Since Alexander was employed at Consolidated Coal Company, a Union operated coal mine, the Union basically owned us. Jenkins, Kentucky was known as a coal camp town, and most of the houses in the hollers were owned by the coal company. Alexander was paid in script which could only be spent in the company stores, so what we had was provided courtesy of the union.

It mattered not to me because I loved my new life. I spent my days wallpapering each of the five rooms and decorating our little love nest with second hand furnishings given to me by neighbors. Hazel helped me make curtains to cover the windows in the kitchen and sitting room, and I hand stitched a patch-work quilt that covered our bed.

Alexander and I spent our evenings talking and laughing and planning our future together. Alexander knew from the start that I wanted children more than anything in the world, as the topic of babies often dominated the conversation. I prayed to the Lord every day for children. I would even get out the Bible I had received when I lived with Aunt Pandy and stare at the clover I placed next to Psalm 127. The Psalm that read: *"Lo, children are an heritage of the Lord: and the fruit of the womb is his reward."* The clover was still intact, and that meant it still contained my wish for babies of my own. I just felt in my heart the Lord would soon answer my prayer.

CHAPTER FORTY-SIX

S pring of 1939 was taking its own sweet time arriving. I was beginning to feel so tired and sluggish myself and thought it was
due to all the dreary, cold days. By mid-April I knew it was more
than the weather making me tired because I was now getting sick
on a daily basis. I knew in my heart that I must be pregnant. I
made an appointment with the company doctor, and he confirmed
my suspicion. I was more than happy; I was elated! I could not
wait to tell Alexander the news.

Following my doctor's appointment, I wanted to tell the whole
world that I was going to have a baby, but I resisted the urge to
tell my family and neighbors because I wanted Alexander to be
the first to know. I went straight home and prepared Alexander's
favorite meal.

I had intended to tell Alexander over supper that I was going
to have a baby, but when he walked in that evening, I could wait
no longer. I met him at the door and blurted out, "We are going
to have a baby!"

I was so overcome with emotion that sobs followed the announcement. We just stood there hugging and crying while our supper set cooling on the table. When I let go of Alexander's neck, he looked down at me and patted my stomach, "Lucy Hornaday is going to be a momma. Now, what about that!"

I grabbed his hand, "I fixed your favorite for supper, chicken and dumplings, so let's eat."

Alexander ate all of his chicken and dumplings and most of mine as my stomach was too full of butterflies to eat. I kept pinching myself the remainder of the evening just as reassurance that this was real.

As soon as I crawled into bed, I said a prayer of thanks because I knew that God had answered my prayer and blessed my womb.

Before falling asleep, I pinched myself one last time. I could hardly believe it was true; I really was going to be a momma!

CHAPTER FORTY-SEVEN

The word traveled like wild fire through the hollers, "Lucy's going to have a baby!" Everyone that knew me knew how much I wanted babies, and everyone seemed excited, too. By late summer, I had hand-stitched a baby quilt using all the pastel colors, so it would be suitable for a boy or a girl. I was really beginning to feel pregnant, as I had begun to feel the baby kicking inside of me.

In late August, Alexander and I moved to Brickyard Hill into a new company house. This house had been built as a duplex. Even though the house was not as big, it was new, and we would have good neighbors.

I got busy decorating our new home, all the while, anticipating our new arrival. By early fall, I was really feeling the effects of my condition, as my legs, hands, and feet began swelling. Each day, before Alexander left for work, he made me promise not to work so hard and to keep my feet propped up, as the doctor had ordered. I obeyed when I could, but I did want the house clean and a proper supper cooked for Alexander each night, and no one could possibly do that with their feet propped. When I did find the time to prop my feet, I would take out my Bible and read aloud the Psalms while I gently rubbed my baby that lay beneath my swollen belly.

By late October, with a due date of mid-December, Alexander and I began trying to sort out a name for our baby. Alexander wanted to name the baby Victor Joe if it was a boy and Ina Sue if it was a girl. I told him about my aversion to middle names. Daddy and Momma gave none of us kids middle names because Daddy so hated his name, Moe Joe Elmore. I told him that middle names just complicated matters and especially for girls. Once married, girls then have four names, but not me because my daddy and momma were smart and simply named me Lucy Elmore, so now I'm Lucy Elmore Hornaday. Alexander was willing to forego the middle name, and we decided on Joe if it was a boy, to honor my daddy, and Sue if it was a girl.

I began decorating for Christmas in late November, as I wanted to have everything ready in case this baby decided to arrive early.

Will sent word that he had gotten married, and he and his new bride, Sarah, were coming to spend Christmas with us. I could not wait to see Will, as it had been years since we had seen each other. I decided that even though space was limited in our new house, this would be the gathering place for the whole family, come Christmas. The week before Christmas I got a burst of energy and spent the whole week baking cookies, making candy, and delivering treat bags all over the holler.

By Christmas Eve, I did not have an ounce of energy left in my body, and I was beginning to feel pains down low in my back. I thought I must have pulled something out of place after walking up and down that holler so many times. I went to bed early on Christmas Eve but was jarred awake in the wee hours of the morning with terrible cramping in my stomach. I woke Alexander and told him that he must get the doctor because I thought I might be having our baby. He returned with Dr. Higgins and, after I was checked, he said that it would be a while and to call him when the pains got closer.

Around daylight, I tried to get up and get ready for all the company that was going to convene here this Christmas evening, but I was stopped in my tracks with the most intense cramps I had ever had. I made my way back to bed, and Alexander pulled up a chair beside me and held my hand. Between the labor pains we talked baby talk.

"What will the baby be, a boy or a girl? Who will he/she look like, you or me? Will he/she be fat or slim?"

I think the anticipation was getting the better of us both.

Around lunchtime, the pain intensified and the contractions were coming faster and lasting longer. I knew it was time for the doctor. The doctor arrived at about the same time my whole family including Will and his new bride convened on our house. The pain was excruciating, but knowing that this pain had a wonderful outcome, a brand new baby, made it all bearable.

At 4:00 Christmas evening I heard the cry of my new baby boy, Joe Hornaday. When the doctor laid him on my stomach to cut the cord, I rubbed his tiny head and looked up toward heaven and whispered, "*Thank you Lord.*"

After everything was cleaned up, Doctor Higgins called for Alexander to come into the room. I will never forget the excitement and love in Alexander's eyes. He held Joe up in the air and proclaimed, "I would like for everyone to meet the future President of the United States."

I could hardly believe that I really had myself a baby and a Christmas baby at that. I thought God has shown favor on me because after coming and getting my momma on Easter he sent me my first baby on Christmas, the same day we celebrate Jesus' birth.

As the evening faded into night, I lay there suckling my new baby boy. I could now sense how Mary must have felt on that first Christmas, and I definitely knew that, just like Mary, I would keep all these things and ponder them in my heart.

CHAPTER FORTY-EIGHT

I lay in bed the entire night holding Baby Joe and studying each intricate detail of his hands, face, and feet. He had the finest blonde hair, the bluest eyes, and the pinkest little lips. He was plump with the fairest, softest skin, and I thought him to be perfect by any standards. I kissed each of his tiny fingers and toes while he slept peacefully.

Alexander, too, seemed to be floating on a cloud. He did manage to get a little sleep, but he roused at every grunt and whimper Baby Joe made.

Our home became a buzz with visitors the following day. Not only my family, but half the holler congregated in our bedroom. The neighborhood women and Bertha were all oohing and aahing over Baby Joe, all the while, spewing out instructions on proper baby care and child rearing. I just smiled and thanked them for their advice, but I thought to myself, I have been planning for this since I was twelve, and the Good Lord has given me enough common sense to see my baby raised.

Bessie stayed with us the next several days, as the doctor had ordered me to complete bed rest for nine days, to give all my internal organs adequate time to return to their proper positions. Staying in bed for nine days was nearly impossible. I could feel my energy returning, and there were so many things that I needed to be up doing. When Bessie and Alexander were out of the house I would sneak out of bed, tend to simple chores, and rock my new baby while he nourished.

I could not believe how much Baby Joe had already changed me emotionally. I felt that I now had a full and total understanding of my momma's quote, *"It's a great life if you don't weaken, but who wants to be strong."*

Baby Joe had completely changed my priorities, and I knew that forever more I would be carrying my heart outside my body. Every decision I made from now on would be based on what is best for him. I now understood how hard it must have been on Momma leaving us behind at such a young age because having Baby Joe gave me a newfound reason to live and a new purpose for my life.

A few days after Joe's birth I reached for my Bible that lay on the nightstand and opened it to Psalms 127 and read: *"The fruit of the womb is his reward."* I gently rubbed the clover that lay pressed between the pages and again thought back to the day I found it and made that special wish for babies of my own. I gazed down upon Baby Joe fast asleep in his cradle, and smiled as I thought about all the brothers and sisters I planned to one day give him.

CHAPTER FORTY-NINE

I took to my role as Momma like butter to bread. It seemed almost second nature to me as Momma had trained me for this from the time Bonnie was born. Even after Momma's death, I had continued to get lots of experience, as I was always taking care of everyone else.

I must have gotten so caught up in having a baby of my very own and keeping my head so far up in the clouds that everything outside Alexander and Baby Joe was just passing me on by without me ever looking around to take notice. I did not even realize that Bonnie had found herself a man until Daddy and Bertha came down to the house the first Friday evening in October and told us that Bonnie was getting married that very weekend and moving to El Paso, Texas to be with her new husband, Nathaniel, who had just been drafted by the US Army.

I knew Daddy did not approve of Bonnie's decision because he sat at our table wringing his hands the whole time Bertha told us everything she knew about Bonnie's fiancé. Daddy interjected,

"I don't want to see Bonnie lose her heart to a man that may lose his life to a war."

I stood behind them in the kitchen, swaying back and forth, with Baby Joe on my hip. I felt a twinge of terror shoot through my body thinking about this war being fought across the ocean and how so many men could lose their lives. I looked at Baby Joe, as he sat on my hip eating a cookie. I could not imagine ever being strong enough to let him go fight a bloody war. I glanced over at Daddy as he sat wringing his hands, "Do you think we are going to be pulled into this war?"

He somberly replied, "It's just a matter of time."

I could only pray that Daddy's prediction would prove wrong because I did not want to even think about Alexander being shipped off to war.

I knew Bonnie must be feeling a whole lot of different emotions right now with Daddy not approving her union and her fixing to up and leave her whole family behind, all the while, forging ahead into unchartered waters.

After Daddy and Bertha left, I felt hard pressed to pay Bonnie a visit. I asked Alexander to watch Baby Joe while I was gone.

When I got to the Johnson's place I could hear Bonnie talking on the back porch. I walked around and saw that she was talking to herself while she hung her white skirt over the line that was tied between the two porch posts. As I walked over to where she stood, I could not help but get teary eyed. Bonnie seemed a ball of nerves, and I knew she was torn because she looked at me and said, "Lucy, I intend to marry Nathaniel even if Daddy says he won't be there. I have to do this now because it may be my only chance since Nathaniel is having to leave the state and may be shipped off to war."

Bonnie looked into my eyes for some type of approval and I responded, "Bonnie, I have never met Nathaniel, but if you feel as strong for him as I do for Alexander, I know it's the right thing. I guess you just need to follow your heart."

I hugged Bonnie, "You go and be happy and bring back lots of babies for us to spoil."

She whispered in my ear, "I do love Nathaniel, but what if he does get killed in this awful war?"

I pulled back and held her at arms' length, "I'm going to tell you just like Daddy use to tell me, 'If you have a bad thought, get it out of your mind as quick as you can.'"

I added, "That advice always worked for me and I know you, Bonnie, are way too head strong to ever let things get you down."

I smiled, "But remember, Bonnie, a way to a man's heart is through his stomach, and I sure hope someone has taught you the proper way to make biscuits."

She chuckled and grabbed me around my waist hugging me tight. "Lucy, I never told you this, but Momma did give you the perfect name because you are always a bright light even in the middle of a dark night."

Bonnie left as Mrs. Nathaniel Jones that very weekend and, even though the family had mixed feeling about her decision, Bonnie was all smiles. I could see in her eyes that she was in love. Daddy stood wringing his hands as they drove out of the holler headed for Texas, but I knew in my heart Bonnie would be just fine.

CHAPTER FIFTY

B y Thanksgiving 1940 Baby Joe had already met his walking milestone. It seemed that he just jumped off my hip one day and went to walking. Once he started there was no stopping him, and it was all I could do to keep him in my sights. He was into everything and more curious than any baby I had ever seen.

I wanted to put up the Christmas tree early for him since this Christmas would be his first birthday. Alexander surprised me the first Friday in December with a beautiful Spruce Pine he picked up on his way home from the coal mine. Alexander brought that tree into the living room, and Baby Joe just cackled. I told him it was a Christmas tree, and he bounced up and down squealing and pointing at the tree propped against the wall.

After Alexander got the tree into its stand, it almost reached the ceiling. I went to the hallway closet and pulled out all the Christmas decorations, and Alexander and I spent the entire evening decorating our beautiful tree. Baby Joe sat in his high chair watching us while he snacked on puffed wheat. When we tossed the tinsel over the branches, Baby Joe banged his high chair and laughed out loud.

After we finished with the decorations, I removed Baby Joe from the high chair and cautioned him not to pull on the tree, but it was like a magnet to him. He crept over and ran his little hand through the bottom branches while he cackled and squealed at an ear piercing frequency.

He loved that Christmas tree! In fact, he loved that tree so much that I was forced to remove it from the sitting room a few days before Christmas for fear that he was going to pull it over on himself. He was always slipping off from me and heading straight for the tree. As he got ever more comfortable with it, he began pulling on its branches harder and harder. I could just see him pulling it over onto himself. To ease my mind Alexander placed our Christmas tree out on the porch, and there it stayed until New Year's Day.

Even with the tree on the porch it still magnetized him. I constantly found him standing in the window looking at that tree perched out on our porch, while he banged on the panes of glass and chattered to his Christmas tree as if it could talk back.

CHAPTER FIFTY-ONE

By the following spring I knew I must be the luckiest woman in the world. Baby Joe was growing and thriving, and to top that off I was going to have another baby. Alexander could not have been happier, and I did not think my life could get any better. Everything seemed so perfect, but I had learned at a very young age the sunny days in your life must be followed by the rain, and in late autumn that rain began to fall.

On November 9, 1941 tragedy struck again. Alexander and I were just getting into bed that Sunday night when we heard a knock on the door. Alexander went to the door, and I could hear a mumbled voice that sounded like my daddy. I heard Alexander say, "No she's still awake; we were just fixing to get into bed."

My heart started pounding, and I immediately grabbed my robe and made my way to the front door. I saw my daddy standing there on the porch with tears welling up in his eyes, wringing his hands. In a very shaky voice, I asked, "Daddy, what's wrong?"

Before he could get out all the words, "Will's been in a near fatal car crash in North Carolina, and I am going there now to check to see if he's still alive," I burst into tears.

I held to my swollen belly as the sobs wretched from deep with-in me. I had always had a special affection for Will, not only was he my only brother, but he looked so much like Momma and had her gentle spirit. I had always felt that as long as he was in the world a part of Momma would stay alive. When I was able to speak I said, "Daddy tell me everything you know."

He replied, "I don't know any details other than he hit a car head on, and he has been transported to a hospital in Lenoir."

He added, "I am leaving now, and I will send word when I know more."

I reached up and hugged Daddy tight. I whispered, "I'll be praying for us all, and let me know as soon as you can."

Daddy kissed my forehead, "Take care of yourself and that baby. I'll send word soon."

I stood out on the porch and watched as Daddy pulled out of the drive. I continued to stand there with the icy wind slicing through my body until Daddy's car lights were completely out of sight.

After returning inside, Alexander and I sat silently on the couch for the longest time while I held tight to his hand.

When we finally made our way back to bed, I pulled the covers over my unborn baby, and I prayed:

"Lord, I realize for every sunny day you have blessed me with I must be willing to accept a rainy one. I am so thankful, Lord, that my sunny days have far exceeded my rainy ones. I'm just asking that you spare Will and give him some more sunny days, too. Daddy needs him here and so do I. Help us, Dear Lord, I pray. Amen."

I lay still for a few minutes, and then began to softly hum my song while Alexander gently stroked my hair, before finally drifting to sleep.

CHAPTER FIFTY-TWO

The next couple of weeks were touch and go with Will. He had survived the crash, but his injuries were extremely serious. He had a broken arm, but worse, a broken back. The break in his back had left him paralyzed from the waist down. Daddy grew increasing unhappy with the care he was receiving at Haven Memorial Hospital because as he put it, "They were just waiting for him to die."

Daddy felt the way he did because the only surgeon at Haven Memorial qualified to do the surgery was unwilling to perform the needed operation on Will's back. According to the doctor, it was way too risky given the severity of the injury.

After a week long search for a neurosurgeon willing to perform the surgery, Daddy got in touch with Dr. Gall, considered by many to be the best in North Carolina. The following day against hospital orders, Daddy checked Will out of Haven Memorial and transported him to Charlotte Regional Hospital.

Two days later Dr. Gall performed the operation. The surgery lasted more than eight hours, but it proved futile. The impact of the car crash had nearly severed Will's spinal cord in two, and there was no way to repair the damage. Dr. Gall explained to Daddy that Will would never walk again and, even worse than that, his spinal cord would eventually work in two which would result in death. He went on to explain that Will could live two minutes or two years he could not say exactly because that would be left up to God's time clock. He did tell Daddy that Will would need round the clock care once he was discharged from the hospital.

Daddy talked to Will and his wife Sarah about moving out to Jenkins to live with Bertha and him. Daddy said he felt it was what was best for Will since most of our family was living in Jenkins, and he and Sarah would have a lot of support in helping with his care. Will and Sarah agreed and on December 6, 1941 they returned to Jenkins.

I'll never forget the day Will came home. There was a dusting of snow on the ground, and I so wanted to put up the Christmas tree to add some cheer. I found this to be impossible because I was ready to give birth any day, and just keeping up with Baby Joe took all my energy. I managed to cook a pot of pinto beans and cornbread and took it up the hill to Daddy's and waited with Bertha until he, Will, and Sarah arrived home.

I peered out the window as Daddy and Sarah got out of the car. Daddy walked around and opened Will's car door. My heart began pounding in my chest, and I could feel my abdomen tighten. I watched as Daddy pulled Will from his car seat. Will looked so frail and helpless, and it was all I could do to hold back the tears as I watched Daddy carry him to the door.

As they entered the house, I mustered a smile and tried to act cheery as I went to give Will a hug, but it was Will who broke the ice. He looked over at Baby Joe and said, "See you're not the only one that can be carried around on someone's hip," and he reached over like he was going to have me take him from Daddy.

Baby Joe saw that Will was reaching for me, and he marched right over to Will and looking up at him said, "No, my momma!"

We all had a hearty laugh which seemed to completely ease all the tension.

After Daddy unloaded all Will and Sarah's things, we all gathered around the table to eat our pinto beans and cornbread. I felt thankful that Will, Bessie, Daddy, and I were all together again and, even though Bonnie was not with us, I knew she was in a happy place and that made everything ok.

CHAPTER FIFTY-THREE

The following afternoon Bertha came down to the house looking like she had just seen a ghost. I just knew something terrible had happened to Will. Before I could ask any questions, she asked if I had heard the news.

I responded, "What news?"

Bertha somberly replied, "Pearl Harbor has been attacked by the Japanese, and thousands are presumed dead."

I felt my stomach clench as I thought back to Daddy's prediction that it would only be a matter of time until we were pulled into the awful war.

The following day Franklin D. Roosevelt declared all-out war on Japan. I could not help but worry about Bonnie and Nathaniel. I prayed Nathaniel would be able to avoid being shipped overseas, as we had just received word that Bonnie was pregnant.

Three days after our nation declared war, the sun began to shine on me again as I gave birth to my second baby boy. On December 11, 1941 Alfred Hornaday was born. My heart melted all over again when I held him in my arms for the first time.

Baby Joe was so excited to meet his new baby brother. Alexander brought him into the room and sat him on the bed beside me as I lay cuddling Alfred. Baby Joe patted my hand. I took hold of his little hand and said, "This is your new baby brother. His name is Alfred."

Baby Joe patted Alfred's tummy, while looking up at me with two year old wisdom and said, "This is OUR baby ain't it Momma, but I'm YOUR baby ain't I Momma?"

He then laid his head over on my lap. I patted his head and reassuringly replied, "That's right, Baby Joe, that's exactly right."

The following day we received word that against all hope Nathaniel was being shipped overseas, and Bonnie was on her way back to Jenkins. Alexander and I decided that Bonnie would stay with us since Daddy and Bertha already had a full house and more on their plate than they could say grace over.

Bonnie could not have come when I needed her worse. Dr. Higgins had again ordered me to nine days of complete bed rest following my delivery and having a two year old made that very difficult. Baby Joe would crawl up in the bed with me and want to sit on my lap and have Alfred sit in our lap. He was definitely a hand's- on big brother, who tried to help with everything, so Bonnie just happened to arrive back in Jenkins at the perfect time.

I remember, on my ninth and final day of bed rest, Baby Joe crawled up on the bed and said, "Me want a Christmas tree."

I explained that we were not going to have a tree this year, but Santa Claus was still coming and bringing all kinds of presents. He looked at me with the saddest eyes, "I'd rather have a Christmas Tree than all the presents, Momma."

I knew that I had to get him a tree. The following day Alexander brought home our tree, and Bonnie decorated it with the help of Baby Joe. True to form, he loved the Christmas tree and tried to tell Alfred all about it.

Even though Will's condition and the uncertainty of this raging war cast a dark shadow over all of our moods, I was determined to make Christmas extra-special for our family. We all gathered at Daddy's on Christmas evening, and I surprised everyone with a special treat.

We all loved ice cream, but most especially Will. I had been experimenting with different recipes that I froze in ice trays. I had evolved my recipe into a rich, creamy concoction that tasted like "pure perfection" as Alexander put it. I made a delicious vanilla ice cream that proved to be a huge hit. It seemed to soothe away all the stress and tension from the events of the past month.

While we all sat around the table eating our ice cream, Will spontaneously burst into song. We all joined him singing, "Jingle Bells." Everyone was laughing and singing and eating "good old home-made ice cream." I must say I wanted to ball this moment up and fasten it securely to my heart forever. It appeared that everyone's cares had melted away, and we were all present in this moment just enjoying each other and all our blessings that remained.

CHAPTER FIFTY-FOUR

Following our Christmas party, Will developed an addiction to my ice cream. I made my frozen concoction every couple of days and delivered Will a fresh batch. Will appeared to be strengthening and his mood brightened. He soon grew attached to my boys and wanted to spend all of his time with them.

I remember one cold, dreary day in the middle of February 1942 when Will offered to watch Alfred while I ran back to the house to check on some newly freezing ice cream. When I returned with a fresh supply for Will, he was sitting in his wheelchair with a noticeable wet spot on his pants. His hands were outstretched holding on to Alfred, who was dangling in mid-air. When Will saw me walk through the door he announced, "Alfred did it, I promise it wasn't me!"

I jokingly said, "Now don't blame that on my innocent little Alfred. You know my pint-sized baby could not pee a whole gallon."

What made the situation even more humorous was Baby Joe's response to Will. I was in the process of potty training Baby Joe, and he looked at Will and said, "You big boy now, you need to go to the potty."

Will grabbed Baby Joe and said, "Are you a big boy?"

Baby Joe nodded yes.

Will let go of Joe and said, "Well, if you are a big boy, we need to stop calling you Baby Joe."

Baby Joe looked over at me, wrinkled his nose and said, "I big boy now, Momma. I not Baby Joe."

I replied, "Alright, we will just call you Joe."

I took Alfred into the bedroom and changed his diaper. Afterwards, I fixed Will a big bowl of strawberry ice cream to make up for Alfred's accident.

Following Alfred's christening of Will, Will would always have me double check his diaper before placing him in his lap.

This episode also had a positive impact on Joe's potty training. Since Will had deemed Joe a big boy, he so wanted to please his uncle. From that day forward, every time we made the trip to Daddy's, Joe would run to find Will and, while showing off his big boy underwear, would announce, "Me big boy, me use the potty."

Will would always clap and make a big deal over his achievement while Joe clapped and squealed with delight.

I could see my babies growing up right before my eyes. I knew I could not hold back time or push it forward; I just had to take it as it comes.

CHAPTER FIFTY-FIVE

March had never been my favorite month, and March 1942 proved to be no exception. Will appeared to be getting stronger, and he felt with some help he could learn to walk again. One afternoon in early March, while we were visiting, Will asked Daddy and Alexander to help him stand up. Daddy and Alexander stood on either side of Will and pulled him to his feet. Will tried and tried to move his feet, but he was unable to take a single step. That single event seemed to be emotionally devastating for Will. He told me a couple of days later that he did not want to live if he could never walk again. I tried to lift Will's spirit by telling him he had sunny days ahead, but he could not see a future without the use of his legs.

Will's overall health seemed to rapidly decline and within a week he came down with a horrible cold that seemed to me the beginning of pneumonia. Daddy sent for Dr. Higgins and he prescribed a chest ointment and cough syrup. Will did not respond to the treatment, and within the week following a horrible coughing spell, he slipped into a coma.

We all took turns sitting with Will, and as I sat with him I would tell him funny stories from our growing up days and the humorous things my boys were saying and doing. I wanted to lift his spirits in hope that it would lift him out of this coma. That hope would not be realized this side of heaven because on March 28th at 12:30am Will went to be with my momma.

I could not believe that just like Momma, Will, too, had been taken at such a young age. In fact, if it had not been for the creation of daylight savings time some two years prior, Will would have died on the tenth anniversary of Momma's death.

We took Will's body back to North Carolina and laid him to rest right beside Momma. Sarah returned to her parent's home in Tennessee, and though we heard from her once in a while, we never saw her again.

Upon our return home from laying Will to rest, I opened my freezer to reveal the ice cream that still set frozen for him. I pulled the ice tray from the freezer and placed it in the sink allowing the faucet water to melt it, and I watched as that melting cream swirled around making pretty patterns and designs as it headed for the drain.

I thought to myself, life is as fragile as this ice cream. Just a minute ago this ice cream was just that- hard, cold ice cream, but this warm water has reduced it to a runny mess. I continued to focus on those patterns and designs forming in the water until they all disappeared down the drain.

I decided that I could be like that ice cream and on days like today when the rain falls leaving me a runny mess I, too, will leave behind a pretty design to help keep me from becoming bitter.

CHAPTER FIFTY-SIX

1942 was a year of change for our entire family, and I tried to adjust to all the changes with a glass half- full attitude.

Will's death took a considerable toll on me, but following his death Bessie up and moved back to North Wilkesboro to work in a hosiery mill. I missed her from the moment she told me she was leaving, but I was glad that she was leaving on her own free will.

By this time, Bonnie was very pregnant and she cried on a nearly continual basis. She was forever complaining that her entire body ached and hurt. She cried over Will's death and Bessie's move, but mostly for Nathaniel who had recently been shipped to Germany.

Bonnie had received a letter from Nathaniel that he was leaving for Germany on an undercover mission since he was fluent in German. He wrote in his letter that he would not be able to write home for the foreseeable future, but welcomed her letters which could be sent to the enclosed address to be forwarded on to him. All the change seemed to weigh on Bonnie, and I knew she was depressed. I tried to pull Bonnie out of her depression, but nothing seemed to work.

One day in early May, I was rocking Alfred, as Joe lay sleeping on the couch. I cracked the window open to get some fresh air. I could hear the birds boisterously singing, but louder still were Bonnie's snubs, as she sat out on the porch penning a letter to Nathaniel. After laying Alfred in his crib, I went outside and took a seat beside Bonnie. I did not say a word; I just sat there listening to her cry. She eventually looked up acknowledging my presence, "What?"

I responded, "We can choose to count our sorrows or count our blessings."

She retorted, "I really don't need your positive outlook right now."

I huffed, "Bonnie Jones, you are carrying in your body a gift from God and that makes you rich, but you don't even know it."

I stood up and walked back inside. I checked on my boys and went into the kitchen to begin cooking supper. I was rolling out the dough to make fried apple pies when Bonnie stepped into the doorway. I turned around and she said, "Could you spare a little of that dough for a ball?"

I laughed, "You bet."

After supper that evening, Alexander sat on the porch tending to Alfred and Joe as Bonnie and I played Dough Ball until dark.

The following month Bonnie gave birth to a beautiful baby boy that she named Russell. Russell was the light at the end of Bonnie's tunnel, and he seemed to be just what she needed to bring her out of her depression.

In early fall, Daddy and Bertha moved back to Wilkesboro, North Carolina. Daddy said it was to get out of the coal mine, but I knew in my heart he wanted to be close to where we laid Will to rest.

Our whole family was struggling through the pain of losing Will, the awful World War, and the family moves. Even though Daddy and Bessie were living two states away, and I was feeling the pain of all the loss and change too, I chose to see the pretty side of life and all that I had to be thankful for. I decided that, instead of focusing on those things that caused me pain, I would keep my sights firmly fixed on my boys, Alexander, and all my many blessings which were too numerous to ever count.

CHAPTER FIFTY-SEVEN

The next year seemed to move along at a fever pitch. I enjoyed every minute with my boys. They were growing up way too fast. Alfred was now walking and talking, and he and Joe kept each other entertained for hours on end. They played so well together that I was able to wallpaper our entire house by summer's end.

Alexander made the comment, one evening, as he watched me take a rag to wipe the excess paste from our bedroom wall where I had hung fresh wallpaper, "If you ever go crazy, I will just put a rag in your hand and let you go to wiping. That should keep you happy all day long."

I slung the rag at him, "If I ever go crazy, I'm just going to take you with me."

He picked me up and tossed me over his shoulder at about the same time Joe came into the bedroom. Joe looked up at Alexander and said, "Where are you taking, Momma?"

Alexander replied, "To go crazy."

Joe's eyes widened as he asked, "Can I go, too, Daddy?"

Alexander said, "Why sure!" We are all about halfway there already."

Alexander put me down, only to pick up Joe and toss him on the bed. Joe squealed and climbed to his feet, jumping up and down on the bed. Alfred soon appeared in the doorway, having been awaken from his nap. Joe said, "Come on, Alfred, we're going crazy."

Alfred crawled up on the bed, where he and Joe jumped and laughed, while I put the finishing touches on my newly papered wall.

I watched my boys as they giggled and played. They were healthy, safe, and happy and that was all I needed in life.

CHAPTER FIFTY-EIGHT

It would not be long before I found myself pregnant for the third time. When I told Alexander he just winked at me, "Well, the third time's the charm."

I knew what he meant. We did want at least one girl, but I would be happy with whatever God laid in my arms.

My third pregnancy was not difficult at all. I was never sick and had tons of energy. I also had an appetite that would not let up. Alexander would kid me about having to work double shifts in the coal mine to support my appetite.

Bessie returned for a visit in the fall of 1944. She brought with her news that she had met the love of her life, Roger Bledsoe. She filled Bonnie and me in on all the details about Roger and his family. She told us that she planned to marry Roger before Christmas.

I was so happy for Bessie. I did not tell her, but I had worried about her since she left Jenkins. I did not like her living in that boarding house, even if it was with kinfolk. I knew first-hand what kinfolk were capable of doing, and I was glad she was well on her way to marital bliss.

I was really glad that Bessie was still with us when I gave birth to my third son, Norman Hornaday on September 12, 1944. I must admit I was hoping for a girl, but when I saw his face and heard him cry for the first time, I was through wishing. I would not have traded him for all the gold in Fort Knox.

Joe and Alfred enjoyed their role as big brothers, and they relieved my feet from much of the fetch work.

I knew early on that Norman had a mischievous streak in him, and I would need to grow eyes in the back of my head to keep him in line. Once he started crawling, he was into everything and he loved more than anything to pull the cat's tail. It made no difference to him how many times I warned him that the cat was going to scratch him if he kept it up, it took the cat actually following through on my warnings before he stopped.

Once Norman started walking there was no stopping him except for his two older brothers who became his judge and jury. I was certain that Joe would grow up to be in law enforcement because he made sure Norman stayed in line, and when things went awry he would always run to find me, so he could tattle on his little brother. It soon became obvious that I did not have to grow those extra eyes in the back of my head because I had Joe seeing everything for me.

CHAPTER FIFTY-NINE

World War II was still raging Christmas 1944. Our little town had certainly not been spared, as we had lost several of our young men to this grueling war, with even more still missing in action. Late Christmas evening, I spotted a strange vehicle pulling into the driveway of our neighbors, Henry and Wilma Blair. I watched as two uniformed officers got out of the car and made their way to their door. My heart ached for the Blair's because I knew the news must be tragic.

I later learned that the plane carrying their son, Winston, had been shot down behind enemy lines, and he was among the missing. I could only imagine how torturous that must be for them.

This news took its toll on Bonnie as well. The stress got to her so bad that she could hardly function. She would almost go into conniptions every time a car was heard heading up the holler. She had terrible nightmares about Nathaniel being tortured in an enemy camp, while she was desperately trying to find him. She would, too often, wake up in a cold sweat gasping for breath.

I fervently prayed every day for Nathaniel's safe return, and I also prayed peace on Bonnie.

May 8th 1945 was the day we all had prayed for so very long. Germany finally surrendered, and it seemed the long war was coming to a welcomed end.

In late July, Bonnie received word from Nathaniel that he was coming home! Nathaniel did not arrive back in the states until late September. He arrived back in Jenkins, on the first day of October, to a celebration that was orchestrated by Bonnie and me. I, too, was ecstatic to see him, as I had watched Bonnie mope and groan for far too long, and I knew Nathaniel was the one to bring her back to life.

Nathaniel and Bonnie soon bought a house in Mudtown and moved out. My boys sure missed Russell, and I did as well, but I was happy that Bonnie had her Nathaniel back, and they could once again be a family.

In short time, after Nathaniel's return, Bonnie was again pregnant. I also received a letter that Bessie and Roger were expecting their first baby.

In July 1946, Bessie gave birth to a bouncing baby boy she named Timmy.

Two months later, in September, Bonnie gave birth to her second son, Spencer.

With ALL of us girls having ALL boys, I thought maybe I should give up on ever having myself a girl because it seemed that only boys ran this Elmore family.

CHAPTER SIXTY

I n late fall 1946 Consolidated Coal Company began selling off some of the houses in the coal camp to offset company expenses. Alexander and I took a particular liking to a two-story, wood frame house located on B & O Hill. We immediately began saving for a down payment. I helped to bring in extra money by selling my homemade ice cream and fudge to neighbors. Every extra cent I could contribute just meant that we could buy our house that much faster.

By early spring, we had finally saved enough money for our initial down payment. On April 30, 1947 we purchased our first home, at 336 B & O Hill, from Consolidated Coal Company for $1,400.00. I could not wait to move into our new home. OUR NEW HOME that we would own out-right, fair and square, in just nine months, after our mortgage was satisfied in full.

That first week in May we began our big move. The boys were as excited as Alexander and I were, and what a big help they proved to be. Joe and Alfred helped me pack up the boxes, and Joe kept his ever-seeing eye on Norman, tattling to me every time he got into some kind of mischief.

I noticed, during our move, that I did not have my usual energy and lost my steam much too quickly. I told Alexander that I thought I was pregnant, and once again Dr. Higgins confirmed my self-diagnosis.

Alexander was again just as excited as I was about the new baby. The boys also wanted a new sibling but quickly informed me that they wanted a sister this time. I, too, wanted a girl, but I was not about to get my hopes up. I told the boys that we would just have to take whatever the stork decided to bring us.

Our new house was much roomier than the rented duplex, but it still had only two bedrooms. I secretly decided to fix a corner of mine and Alexander's room for our new addition, if it so happened to be a girl. I did not even discuss this with Alexander, as I did not want to jinx myself. I placed the cradle on a bright yellow rug in one corner of our room and left the remaining space empty. I had decided, if we did have a girl, I would make that area of the room hers and have Alexander create a privacy partition when she was older.

We could not have been any happier with our new home. Bonnie and Hazel helped me make new curtains, and I pasted new wallpaper on every wall. I really could not believe how wonderful my life was. I had myself a family of my own, and we now had a home of our own. I thought to myself, Hazel was right, it had not taken a high school education to make my dreams come true, and it really seemed that all my dreams were just falling into place.

CHAPTER SIXTY-ONE

December 1947 was well on its way to making the history books as being one of the coldest ever, and I was about to make family history of my own. On December 16th I gave birth to a brand new baby girl. I gave my daddy his very first granddaughter.

Even though she weighed only seven pounds, she proved a difficult delivery, and I never dreamed such a tiny girl could cause me such struggle. The boys were outside my room sitting on the steps, and I could hear them rustling about. I tried my best to keep the intense pain contained for fear that my cries would scare them. I did let out a low moan when she finally made her grand debut. Dr. Higgins smiled, "Lucy, you've got yourself a girl."

I raised my head, "Let me see."

I could hardly believe my eyes, "Dr. Higgins, You're right!"

He laughed, "Well, I've delivered enough that I should know."

I hollered out to Alexander and the boys, "It's a girl!"

Alexander came into the room and Dr. Higgins handed him our baby. He took her in his arms and held her like she was an expensive china doll.

I giggled, "You can hold her like you held the boys; she won't break. I can tell you right now she is tough as nails."

Alexander smiled, "She's just so tiny and delicate."

I took hold of her tiny foot, "Can you believe it Alexander! We now have our Sue, Little Sue Hornaday."

Alexander kissed my forehead, "You did good, Lucy. You did real good."

The boys soon piled into the room, as they were all eager to love on their new baby sister.

Later in the evening, Bonnie came down to make certain for herself that I indeed had a girl. She winked when she unpinned her diaper, "I should have known if any of us Elmore girls could do it, it would be you."

I smiled back at her and wrinkled my nose, "I would have been just as happy with a boy, but I'm sure glad I got my girl. Don't you give up Bonnie, and you'll get yours too."

Bonnie stayed until way after dark and helped Alexander get our boys in bed. She came back into the room and asked if she could get me anything.

I smiled, "Could you make me a cornbread cake before you leave?"

She nodded and left the room. She soon appeared with a sizzling hot cornbread cake topped with butter. She peered down at me, "You're thinking about Momma aren't you, Lucy?"

"Yeah, Bonnie I guess I am. Thanks for everything, you're the best."

Bonnie touched her forehead to mine, "Sleep well, and I will be back in the morning."

As I sat in bed savoring my cornbread cake, Sue began to fuss. I reached over and pulled her to my chest. As she began to nurse

I started to hum my song. I could feel how Momma must have felt that first evening as she lay cuddling me. Having Sue made me realize how much I, too, needed a daughter, but not in the same way Momma needed me. I needed her to make our family complete.

CHAPTER SIXTY-TWO

Christmas 1947 was the most perfect thus far. Even though we did not get to spend Christmas with our extended family, I had my three boys and my baby girl, and by all accounts my life was as sweet as sugar. Alexander and I could not believe how richly God had blessed us.

By the first of the year, work began to slow down in the mines, and Alexander was allowed to work the graveyard shift to secure more hours. Despite the slow-down we were able to make our final payment to Consolidated Coal Company on January 31, 1948, and we now held the deed for 336 B & O Hill.

I did not want to love our home too much because I knew how quickly fire could destroy it along with our worldly possessions. Even though I was not willing to openly admit it, I was scarred by the tragedy of losing my childhood home. I never wanted for anything more than what we needed and only wanted the necessary household furnishings. I chose instead to spend our money on the very best food for our kids. In my mind this was a win/win situation. I could give my children the proper nutrition necessary for them to grow up healthy and strong, and, if by some misfortune I was again faced with our house burning down, we could all grab our food and eat it as fast as we could, limiting our lose to the fire.

Alexander was all too familiar with my unnatural fear of fire. In our new home, we heated with a Warm Morning Stove that was fueled by coal. The stovepipe would often times turn red as the temperature of the fire intensified. Every time the stove pipe turned red, I would begin whooping, hollering, and dancing all around while begging Alexander to do something to cool the stove pipe. He would always laugh and tell me I sounded like a fire engine, all the while reassuring me that the fire was fine.

I think he grew weary after weeks and weeks of bone chilling cold weather and having to almost constantly reassure me of the fire's safety because one afternoon he came home with a fire "stingerisher." I never could pronounce extinguisher and Alexander got the biggest kick out of my attempts to properly pronounce it. Alexander hung that "stingerisher" in the sitting room on the wall opposite the heater. He explained that if a fire did indeed escape that stove pipe the "stingerisher" would take care of it. It did give me some reassurance, but I still never offered to feed the fire when Alexander was working.

CHAPTER SIXTY-THREE

Early spring I got into my head that I wanted to raise a few chickens for the eggs, since we now held the deed for our land. I told Alexander about my idea. He rebutted, "Lucy, a handful of chickens will be more trouble than their few eggs will be worth."

I winked, "We'll see."

I had already set my sights on the six baby chicks the Pine Store was giving away to one lucky winner on Good Friday. For the first three Fridays in March, I made my way to the Pine Store and made the minimum $2.00 purchase to enter my name in the drawing. The following Friday I made certain to be at the store in time for the drawing. Old Man Jennings pulled the name from the box and cleared his throat before announcing, "The winner is Lucy Hornaday."

I could not believe my ears. I was so excited that I ran straight home to tell Alexander leaving my crate of chicks behind. Alexander was not as excited, but I explained, "They will be Easter chicks for the kids and later on a fresh supply of eggs for us."

He hesitantly agreed to build me a small chicken coop when my chicks outgrew the crate.

Joe overheard us talking and came running. "You mean we have Easter chicks. Where, Momma?"

I already knew that Joe would be the most excited. He had always been drawn to nature and possessed an instinctive love for animals. I pushed back the hair from my eyes, "I left them at the Pine Store, and I'm going back to fetch them now."

Joe was not about to let me return alone. In fact, he had all those chickens named before we made it back to the house.

Alexander was out back upon our return, already working on my chicken coop. He just rolled his eyes at me and said, "Women, who can figure them out! One day they want babies and the next they want diddles."

I reached up and tapped his head, "You'll be happy about this come Thanksgiving when a big, fat, roasted chicken is sitting in the middle of the table."

Alexander just smiled and went back to work on the coop.

I set the chicks on the back stoop and told Joe he could be in charge of tending to them. He and Alfred sat out on the stoop all evening loving and petting on those diddles until bedtime.

Unfortunately, the new wore off fairly quickly, as those little diddles were soon young chickens, losing all their cuteness and appeal.

I, too, became increasingly unhappy with my new venture, as these chickens were eating massive amounts of scraps and mash, but were producing no eggs. I soon realized that I was not suited to farming because the smell and mess they left behind were getting the better of me, not to mention, all the crowing. I eventually learned the reason for the lack of eggs- I was the owner of Six Roosters! I did not dare say a word to Alexander about my discontentment because I knew he would just say, "I told you so."

I must say, I was not at all disappointed when the kids and I returned home from a trip with Bonnie to Pikeville, in early fall, to find the chickens had disappeared from the coop. I knew Alexander found them a new home while we were gone, but I never mentioned those chickens and neither did he. It was as if those chickens had never existed.

CHAPTER SIXTY-FOUR

That fall, after Joe and Alfred returned to school, I started my usual quilting when I could make the time. Bonnie had just found out that she was going to have another baby, and I set in to making her a baby quilt. All that sewing conjured up memories of days gone by. I was starting to miss Daddy and Bessie something fierce. It felt like forever since we had seen one another. I decided that a letter to Daddy was long overdue, so I got out my pen and paper and composed a letter:

November 6, 1948 (Saturday Night)
Dearest Daddy and Bertha,
I just couldn't go to bed until I wrote you a line or two. It is 10:30pm now. Alexander has just gotten back from church. The kids are all asleep and I have just finished ironing. Bonnie is just fine, but she has had some morning sickness. Bonnie Bee is about the same, but she has a girl staying with her now since Russell has gone to West Virginia to get a job. Times sure look pretty bad around here. All the mines are on a two week vacation/strike.

Joe and Alfred are making real good grades in school. They haven't missed any yet, and I sure hope they won't have to miss. Sue is as cute as she can be. She says paw-paw. Norman is always writing you both a letter.

Alexander bought me a twin tub washing machine. I guess you have seen them. It is two washings in one. It is supposed to last ninety-nine years. I told Alexander I guess that would be one I wouldn't wear out. (Ha ha)

I would give anything if you all would come out to see us for Thanksgiving or Christmas. It seems like it has been so long since I saw you.

Did you farm a lot this year? Sure hope you aren't working too hard. I got a sweet letter from Bessie last week. They were all well, but it sure made me miss everyone. Tell everyone hello and please visit soon.

Love,

Lucy and Family

(Taken from actual letter)

Daddy and Bertha were unable to make the trip out to Jenkins that winter, so Bonnie and I decided to take all the kids to visit Daddy the following April when the kids had a break from school. Alexander and Nathaniel bought us bus tickets for our one week trip back to Wilkesboro, North Carolina.

Even though Bonnie was seven months pregnant, we decided to leave no stone unturned on this trip. We intended to visit our home place, where the house once stood, and all the landmarks from our childhood. We also wanted to spend as much time with Bessie and Daddy as possible.

The night before our anticipated trip I did not sleep a wink. My mind was racing, and my stomach was full of butterflies. I had so much on my mind. I had never traveled this far with all my children before, not to mention, never having spent one night away from Alexander.

Alexander drove me to the bus depot the following morning where we met Bonnie and her boys. The bus was already filling up when we arrived, and all three of my boys followed Bonnie to the back to sit down. When I stepped on the bus, I noticed that there were no seats left in the back, and I was forced to sit up front holding Sue on my lap. A young soldier boy took the seat across the aisle from me. I assumed that he was on his way home from service.

Once our bus left the station I put a bottle in Sue's mouth and began to gently rock her to sleep. The soldier boy across from me kept fidgeting around in his seat. I knew he was all excited about something. He soon struck up a conversation, telling me all about his last six weeks of basic training, and his anticipation of return-ing home to Abingdon, Virginia. He explained that he was so ex-cited because he had a girl waiting on him, and they were getting married soon.

I was telling him about our trip out to North Carolina to see my daddy and sister. I noticed he kept looking around to the back of the bus. I just kept talking until he stopped me in mid-sentence, "You see all those little cotton-tops sitting in the back? Every one of them is puking."

I turned around and saw all five boys huddled around Bonnie puking their guts out. I didn't let on like I even knew who they were. Bonnie could handle it. I just continued the conversation where I had left off, when he once again interjected, "You see that strawberry blonde sitting back there with all those cotton-tops? Now, she is puking too."

I could not help but get tickled, and Bonnie must have wit-nessed my laughing between heaves because she let me have it out of both barrels when we finally reached the Abingdon depot.

After the bus was hosed down and swept out, we re-boarded for Wilkesboro. To keep Bonnie's anger at bay, once we re-boarded I, too, sat in the back, with all our sick boys, and endured the continual heaving all the way to Wilkesboro. Even though I never threw up, I was sure green around the gills when we finally reached our destination.

Daddy picked us up at the bus depot. He kept commenting on how well behaved the boys were. Little did he know that all their energy had been left behind on the floorboard of that bus. They all were sound asleep by seven o'clock, and Bonnie and I were not far behind. Daddy kept asking if we were all coming down with colds. I told him we were all just tuckered from the trip and spared him all the details.

What a difference a day can make! We all woke up free from our motion sickness and ready for a big breakfast. I told Bertha if she would show me around the kitchen I would do the cooking. When we sat down at the table it was just like old times. Bessie, Bonnie, and myself were gathered with all our children and Daddy. For a minute, I just closed my eyes and relished the moment. After we all finished eating, I began clearing the table. Daddy walked over to me and said," Lucy, you cook just like your momma."

I smiled up at him, "Thanks, Daddy."

Bertha must have overheard Daddy's comment because she cleared her throat and announced, "Now, tonight I am going to make my signature chicken and dumplings. Moe says it's the best meal he ever sunk a tooth in."

I was way too familiar with Bertha's chicken and dumplings, and I must admit I would be hard pressed to ever stick a tooth into that "signature dish."

That night we all gathered at the supper table for Bertha's "signature meal." We all watched as Bertha set the dumplings on the table, with those yellow chicken feet floating in the gravy, and Joe began to cry. He looked over at me, "Is that one of our chickens, Momma?"

"Absolutely not! Our chickens flew the coop. Bertha bought these chicken feet at the store."

With tears dripping off his chin, he cried, "I don't like for chickens to not have feet, and I don't want to eat one."

I could feel everyone's eyes on me. "You don't have to eat the feet, Joe, but you can try a dumpling."

Then he said, "But you go first, Momma."

I could feel my face getting all flushed. "Ok, Joe, I will."

I dipped into the bowl and placed a small dumpling in the center of my plate. I dipped back into the bowl for Joe's dumpling and then Alfred's and Norman's.

Norman begged for a chicken foot on his plate because he wanted to see how sharp the claws were.

I must say that meal was more like a science lesson, with all five boys asking all sorts of questions about those doggone chicken feet. All the explaining and grabbing hands out of the dumpling bowl kept me from ever having to take a taste. As soon as the boys were finished eating, I began scraping their scraps into my plate to prevent Bertha from seeing my untouched dumpling and getting her feelings hurt.

With Bertha's famous chicken and dumplings now out of the way, I got the pleasure of cooking for our families the remainder of the week. The week flew by, and the boys had such a good time running and playing together. Bonnie and I visited all our favorite childhood spots. We even returned back to Cotton Mill Hill but did not venture down because Bonnie was certain she could never climb back up that hill in her current condition.

The morning of our departure Daddy drove us back to the bus station. When the boys saw the bus and heard its diesel engine crank, they began to cry. They pleaded with Daddy to take us back home in his car. Joe looked at me and said, "Is it too far to walk, Momma?"

Norman took hold of his stomach, "Momma, my belly hurts."

I knew we were in for a rough trip home. As soon as Norman set foot on the bus, he began heaving. I recognized the driver from our previous trip, and he immediately recognized us because he began shaking his head and banging it on the steering wheel as we all boarded.

We all took seats in the very back of the bus. Before we even made it out of Wilkesboro, every one of us went to puking. We made a stop in Abingdon, Virginia and once again the bus was hosed and swept out. I think our driver had had all of us he could take because a new driver boarded for the second half of the trip. By the time we arrived home, three-fourths of those riding were throwing up with us. It was a "puke party" of massive proportions. I could not wait to get my feet on stable ground.

Alexander and Nathaniel were waiting for us when we pulled into the bus station. We all staggered out of the bus, and I walked over to the bench beside the sidewalk and sat down. Alexander walked over, and he knew something was wrong. "Everyone getting off that bus looks as green as a gourd. And you, Lucy, look the greenest."

I cupped my face in my hands and gently rocked myself back and forth to ease the nausea. Once my stomach started to settle I looked up at him and said, "Let's just say none of us will ever forget our first bus trip."

Norman looked up at Alexander and said, "I don't like that bus, it makes my belly hurt."

Alfred and Joe nodded in agreement.

Alexander grinned, "Well, I don't guess I have to worry about my best girl venturing off again anytime soon."

I grabbed hold of his hand, "If you are talking about another bus trip, well, I've been there, done that!"

CHAPTER SIXTY-FIVE

Two months after our infamous bus trip Bonnie gave birth to a baby girl. I was outside hanging my wash on the line when I heard an awful commotion. I peeked around the limp, wet sheets and spotted Mrs. Fletcher, our neighbor from across the holler. She was running toward our house with her hands flailing around above her like she had gotten "caught up in the spirit" or something. As she got closer, I could detect that she was calling my name. I walked from behind the bed sheets while waving my hand in the air, "I'm over here, Mrs. Fletcher. Is something wrong?"

She was obviously excited taking in great gulps of air as she spoke, "I just got word that Bonnie is having her baby, right now as we speak, and you need to go be with her. I will watch your young'uns till Alexander gets back."

I took off running as fast as my legs would carry me, and when I walked through the door, I could hear the cries of a brand new baby. I sat down in the ladder back chair next to Bonnie's bedroom and waited for the doctor to emerge. When he stepped out he announced, "It's a girl!"

Nathaniel and I walked into the room to find Bonnie, obviously exhausted from her long labor, but managing a sweet smile as she rose up in the bed and said, "I did it, Sis. I had me a girl, too."

I responded, "Well, let me check to make sure."

She laughed as I pulled back the blanket and winked, "Well, I reckon you did Bonnie. Have you picked out a name?"

She looked over at Nathaniel and back at me and said, "Yes, to tell you the truth Bessie helped me pick out her name on our recent visit. We were outside picking violets to put on the supper table while you were inside cooking, Lucy. I was talking about my hopes of having a girl, and Bessie said, 'Well, I think if you have a girl you should name her Violet.'" I have thought about that ever since, and now that I see her I know that's what her name should be."

I smiled at her, "That's the perfect name because she looks delicate like a violet."

Bonnie then locked her eyes on me and said, "Lucy, please get word to Bessie about my Violet, and let her know that two of us Elmore girls have made history, and now it's her turn to have a girl."

I leaned down and kissed her forehead, while gently rubbing Violet's head. "I will send word to her today and let her know that the ball is now in her court."

Bonnie smiled, "Momma would be proud of us, Sis."

I turned around and looked at Bonnie through the dresser mirror on the opposite wall. "Momma is proud of us Bonnie, and I'm sure she is telling Will all about Violet even as we speak."

CHAPTER SIXTY-SIX

Shortly after Violet's birth, Bonnie and her family moved to Dunham about fifteen minutes away by car. I babysat for Bonnie while she and Nathaniel packed up everything and got settled in their new home. Having Violet around made me yearn for a new baby, too. Sue was already two years old, and I thought she might like to have a baby sister. I expressed my wishes to Alexander who just smiled his crooked smile and winked, "We'll see."

I knew Alexander would eventually give in to my yearning.

The very night, after I brought up the idea of having another baby, I had a terrible nightmare. In my dream, I had just found out that I was pregnant, and upon returning from the doctor visit I found Alexander working on the roof. I yelled up to him, "Can you believe it, I'm pregnant!"

The news so startled him that he slipped on the metal roof and fell to the ground while I watched. I stood frozen with fear as I watched him tumble head first off the roof. I saw the terror in his eyes as gravity forced him toward the ground. Then, at a deafening pitch, his neck snapped when his face slammed into the hard earth. I was immediately jolted awake and sat straight up in the bed. I was overcome by that terror you sometimes get after having a nightmare, and Alexander was at work in the mine and could not comfort me. I did not sleep another wink the remainder of the night. I could hardly wait for morning and to see Alexander walking across the hill from the mine.

At the crack of dawn, I made myself a cup of coffee and went out on the porch. I sat and worriedly watched for Alexander. When I finally caught a glimpse of his silhouette walking across the hill, a feeling of absolute relief flooded over me. I ran to meet him and hugged him tight, "Don't ever leave me. Please, please promise me that."

Alexander took my face in both hands and with concern in his eyes said, "Lucy, what has brought all of this on?"

"I really don't want to talk about it, but I had a terrible dream, and it was about you."

He gently stroked my hair and whispered, "Don't you worry, Lucy, I am not planning on going anywhere, at least not anytime soon."

He smiled his devilish smile and briskly kissed my forehead. "What's for breakfast? I just finished cutting sixteen tons so what do I get?"

I teasingly remarked, "I guess another day older and hungrier than heck. So tell me, what is your stomach in the mood for?"

"I was hoping for fried bologna, gravy, and your homemade biscuits."

I took hold of his hand, "Consider it done!"

After breakfast, Alexander went upstairs to rest, and I got the boys off to school. I grabbed an apple out of the fruit bowl and a spoon from the dish drainer and took Sue out on the porch. I sat her in my lap and began scraping the apple for her to eat.

For some unknown reason, I could not get the nightmare out of my mind. I kept seeing Alexander fall and his neck snap over and over in my mind. I remembered Daddy's saying, "If you have a bad thought get it out of your mind as quick as you can."

As hard as I tried to adhere to Daddy's advice, the more I thought about the dream. I knew the only way to ever get this horrible dream out of my mind was to talk about it. I did not want to tell Alexander because I was afraid of jinxing him so I decided to pay Hazel Painter a visit. I walked across the holler to Hazel's and found her outside hoeing her small vegetable garden. I called out to her, "Hazel, can I talk to you about something that is really eating at me?"

She immediately stood her hoe against the fence post. "Well, I reckon you can. Want to go inside?"

Hazel led the way into the house and on into the kitchen. I sat down at the table while she poured us both a glass of ice cold tea. Once she took her seat, I told her all about the disturbing dream and how the images had haunted me all day. I explained that I felt if I could talk about it I could somehow get it out of my mind.

Hazel assured me that it was only a dream and nothing more, but for some reason I had this uneasy feeling that the dream was preparing me for another rain storm in my life.

CHAPTER SIXTY-SEVEN

Over the next several days, the awful nightmare seemed to fade from my mind, and I thought less and less about that terrible dream. Life seemed to be pushing on at an even pace as summer began to set in. I often thought to myself, where on earth does time go? It was already late June, and summer would be gone before we could even blink an eye.

Alexander and I had plans to meet Bonnie and Nathaniel this last June weekend and take all the kids on a family picnic. When I kissed Alexander and sent him off to work late Thursday night, I had no thought that my life was again about to change.

I went to bed anticipating our upcoming family picnic. I fell asleep almost immediately but was soon startled awake by the voice of Margaret Mounce on my front porch. I heard her say Alexander's name and something about being dead. I thought for a moment that I was dreaming, and this was all part of the dream. Then I heard banging on my front door and again the voice of Margaret Mounce screaming, from behind the closed door, "Lucy, Alexander's dead! Alexander's dead! Alexander's dead!"

I did not even bother to get on my bathrobe. I ran and flung open the door to find Margaret still screaming, "ALEXANDER'S DEAD!"

It's hard to explain exactly how I felt. A numbing sensation began to envelope me, starting at the top of my head and working its way down my body, and I began to violently shake, as if I was freezing, but I was not cold. I grabbed hold of Margaret and shushed her because I did not want to wake up the kids. I was in such shock and so numb that a single tear did not escape my eye, but my legs began to buckle under me, and I crumpled to the couch. I wanted to ask, "How do you know he's dead? What happened? "... but the words would not escape my voice box.

I must have sat on that couch all crumpled for more than fifteen minutes when Charles Teague, a fellow miner, stepped up on the porch, taking off his hat. I knew then that Margaret's news was true, Alexander was dead.

Charles walked through the door and said, "Lucy, I have some really bad news. Alexander was working the coal cutter tonight and hit a seam of hard rock. The rock did not give and it caused the machine to shift, which pinned Alexander against the wall and crushed him. The accident happened at 12:30am. He was already dead before we could get him out of the mine. I'm terribly sorry, Lucy. Please let me know if you need anything and know that you will be in my prayers."

At that moment the tears began to flow like floodgates being raised, and I could not hold back the sobs. I instantly thought back to my nightmare, and I now knew that dream had been my warning.

Margaret stayed with me until Bonnie arrived after daylight. When I saw Bonnie I burst into tears again. I hugged her tight. "We were supposed to go on our picnic tomorrow. Why, Bonnie, oh, why, did this have to happen?"

Bonnie remained silent and just squeezed me tighter.

I eventually composed myself and went into the kitchen to cook breakfast for the kids. I did not know exactly how I was going to break the news to them, but I knew I had to stay strong while in their presence.

When I had them all gathered at the breakfast table, I cleared my throat and began, "I have something to tell you. Your daddy went to heaven last night, and he is going to picnic with Jesus this Saturday."

Joe looked at me with fearful eyes, "You mean Daddy's dead?"

"Yes, Joe, your daddy is in heaven."

Joe's lip began to tremble and Alfred and Norman began to whimper and cry. Sue jumped to the floor, walking into every room while hollering, "Daddy, Daddy, where are you Daddy?"

I had no idea how to properly get a handle on the situation. I felt like that frightened eleven year old girl, losing my momma all over again.

After breakfast, Joe and Alfred went outside to play. It was not long before Alfred came through the back door crying. I ran to the door as Alfred came limping through the kitchen. He was holding his foot, "That block hurt my foot, Momma."

I took off his shoe and kissed the top of his foot, already showing signs of bruising, while he told me about picking up the cinder block and dropping it on his left foot. I scooped him into my arms and held him tight against my chest.

A few minutes later, Joe came into the house with blood streaming down his legs. I put Alfred down and went to find out what happened to Joe. He informed me he had been practicing his home plate slide in the gravel over at the slate dump. I washed the blood from his legs to reveal impaled shins and knees. I pulled him to me, "Did you not know that sliding in the gravel would skin your knees, Joe?"

He moaned, "Yeah, but I was hurting already."

I realized that Alfred and Joe were physically hurting themselves to help mask all the emotional pain they were feeling. I did
not know how to talk to them about what had just happened to
their daddy, and I was so emotionally drained myself that I just sat
on the floor with my arms wrapped around the two of them, humming my song, as I rocked them back and forth. I tried so hard
to contain the tears, but they streamed down my face like a river
and onto my lap. Alfred reached up and wiped a tear from my eye,
"Don't cry, Momma, I love you."

Joe stood up and hugged me tight around the neck, "I'm big,
Momma, and I can take care of us all."

I hugged them both tight, and wiping away the tears I said, "We
will all be just fine. I have you kids, and that's all I need."

Just like Momma's death, I don't remember much about
Alexander's wake and funeral. My only clear memory is of placing
the half-heart that I had given him so many years ago into his shirt
pocket. I held the other half in my hand rubbing the smooth metal between my thumb and forefinger. I had lost the love of my life.

Despite this terrible tragedy, I knew my blessings still out-
weighed my burdens and woes. I had been blessed with precious
children, and had it not been for Alexander, I would have never
been given these four wonderful gifts.

CHAPTER SIXTY-EIGHT

B essie stayed with me for two weeks following Alexander's death. I insisted that she drive me to Wise, Virginia to see Alexander's grave every day. I would stand at the foot of his grave and stare into the small grave marker at its head that read Alexander O'Neil Hornaday, September 18, 1908- June 23, 1950. It all seemed a bad dream- one in which there was no escape. I secretly wondered how I would ever raise four small children alone. For those first few days following Alexander's death, I followed Bessie around the house but was incapable of taking care of my normal chores. I tried my hardest to put my best foot forward around the kids. I wanted more than anything for them to feel secure.

Twelve days after Alexander died, I received a visit from Alexander's brother Von and his wife, Leedy, who lived in Charlottesville, Virginia. Bessie was still staying with me but had taken the boys and walked down to the Pine store to get a sack of meal. I was right in the middle of getting Sue to sleep when they arrived. I invited them into the sitting room and took my seat in the rocking chair with Sue drowsily finishing up her afternoon bottle. I could tell by the way Leedy kept fidgeting with her pocketbook, and Von kept stammering to make small talk that they were not here to merely console me. After several minutes of extreme awkwardness, Leedy put her pocketbook by her side and just blurted out, "Lucy, I know how hard this must be on you with these four small kids, and we have come to try to help ease your burden. We are willing to take Sue and raise her as if she were our own. You know we have the means to give her the finest things and send her to the best schools. Now, we don't want an answer today, but think about it, Lucy. You know it would be in her best interest."

She reached for her pocketbook and opened it taking out a pamphlet. "We also want to give you information on the Children's Home in Richmond, Virginia. We think it would be a good alternative for your boys."

Leedy passed the pamphlet to Von, and he handed it to me. I managed to hold back the tears and politely responded, "If you don't mind showing yourselves to the door, I have to tend to Sue now."

Leedy and Von headed for the door, when all at once, Leedy hesitated and looked back, "Now you think about all this, Lucy. You know what a struggle you would have raising all four of them yourself. It's the best thing you can do for you and your kids."

I smiled, "Thanks for all your concern."

I watched as Von backed their brand new 1950 Packard out of my driveway. I thought to myself, it must be nice to have the world by the tail and all the money to go with it.

I looked down at Sue, her eyes too heavy to stay open. I gently rubbed her hair and began to hum my song to her. I knew firsthand what it was like growing up without a momma, and I was not about to give up my kids without a fight.

CHAPTER SIXTY-NINE

I did not mention Von and Leedy's visit to Bessie when she returned from the store. I needed time to process everything. Leedy's words resounded over and over in my mind. The more I thought about that conversation the more scared I became. I wondered if everyone thought I was incapable of raising my children alone. I did not have any work skills, was two months shy of an eighth grade education, and I wondered how I could ever raise these children into adulthood all by myself. Bessie managed to get all the kids into bed early that night and I was not long behind. I crawled into our bed that now seemed so big and so cold. I pulled my Bible from the nightstand and placed it on my lap. I opened it to the Psalm that sheltered my clover pressed between its pages. I closed my eyes and softly breathed that Psalm: *"Lo, children are an heritage of the Lord: and the fruit of the womb is his reward."*

I thought back to those days when I prayed so hard for children and how God had blessed me with four. I gingerly picked up the fat clover that had grown brittle over time, and I gently pressed it between my index finger and thumb. I knew when I found the clover it was big enough for multiple wishes. Holding tight to the clover, I closed my eyes and prayed:

"Lord, you have seen me though all the tough times in my life, and some of those times were really scary for me, but none as scary as now. You know my circumstances, along with all my weaknesses. I have no idea how I can provide for these four kids you blessed me with, but I do know that I want to be able to do that more than anything. Please show favor on me and my kids. I need your help in keeping my family together. Please lead me in the right direction, keep me firmly planted in your will, and help me to forever keep my bright light shining. It's in your name I pray, Amen."

I opened my eyes and laid the clover back over the Psalm. I closed my Bible and laid it on the bed beside me. I pulled the covers around me and laid my hand over on my Bible; in no time I was fast asleep.

I must have slept like a rock because Bessie already had the boys dressed and fed before I even regained consciousness. I woke up with my Bible still at my side and the verse: *"I will never leave you or forsake you,"* resounding in my mind.

I got dressed and joined Bessie in the kitchen. I made myself a cup of coffee and took a seat at the table. All three boys were scrambling to get outside to play. Bessie cleaned all the dishes from the table and sat down across from me. I looked right into her eyes and said, "Do you think I am capable of taking care of these kids by myself?"

Bessie gave me a puzzled look, "What do you mean? Do you not feel capable?"

"It's not that I don't feel capable, but my ability is certainly coming into question."

What are you talking about, Lucy?

"Well, Von and Leedy paid me a visit yesterday, and they wanted me to give them Sue to raise, and send the boys to an orphanage."

Bessie flew mad. "If that doesn't take the cake! Who died and made them judge and jury?"

"I guess Alexander."

Bessie's mood softened, "I didn't mean it like that, Lucy. What I meant was that they need to keep their noses in Charlottesville taking care of their own business. Lucy, think about it. Who has been taking care of these kids for the last eleven years?"

"I have with Alexander's support."

"Well, that support is gone now, Lucy, and you are left like Daddy was left with us four, so what do you want to happen?"

"Bessie you know that I want more than anything to keep my family together, but I don't know what I am going to do for work. I need a job today to support these kids."

Bessie reached across the table and took my hand, "Lucy, you took care of me, Bonnie, and Will after Momma died, and you were only eleven years old yourself. You took my part when Bertha came down on me, and you protected me from Albert. You, Lucy, are the strongest person I know, and you will find a way to support your kids. It may not be easy, but you will do it."

I squeezed Bessie's hand. "I will do it Bessie. With the help of God I know I will find a way."

CHAPTER SEVENTY

A fter Bessie returned to North Carolina, the reality of losing Alexander began to take hold. I immediately moved Sue to Alexander's spot in our bed. I just could not take sleeping alone. I spent the rest of the summer taking care of all the legal business that goes along with losing a spouse and tending to my four kids. I struggled with intense nightmares of family and sometimes complete strangers jerking my kid's right out from under my arm and hauling them off to an orphanage while they screamed for me, and I stood helpless.

Late summer, I paid a visit to Judge Ormond in Whitesburg, Letcher's county seat. I made the trip to finish closing out Alexander's estate, and as destiny would have it, I was granted the opportunity to talk to the judge. I explained my situation to him and asked him point blank if I would be allowed to raise my own kids. His brow furrowed, and I could see his lips purse behind his wiry mustache as he said to me, "Mrs. Hornaday, do you love your children?"

I spewed, "More than anything! I wanted children from the first time I can remember."

Still stern faced he asked, "Do you have means to provide for your children?

"That's why I am here today. I have finished closing out Alexander's estate. We own our home outright, the children will be getting a small survivor pension, and I am planning to go to work as soon as school starts. Judge Ormond, I will do whatever it takes to feed and clothe my children. They are my whole life, and I could not live and breathe one minute without them."

His look softened, and I could see a smile forming behind that gray coat of hair on his upper lip, "Why, Mrs. Hornaday, you are as capable of taking care of those children as any Children's Home. Now, you just quit all your worry about that."

He reached out and shook my hand. I took his hand in both of mine, and with a firm grip, I shook it like I had shaken no other. I felt like a weight had been lifted off me. If Judge Ormond thought I was fit, well, I was not going to worry about it anymore.

That evening after returning home I fixed pinto beans, fried potatoes, and cornbread cakes for supper. I felt the first spark of happiness since Alexander's death. As those cornbread cakes sizzled in that iron skillet, I smiled because I knew that I now had Alexander, along with Momma and Will, our three guardian angels, watching over us.

CHAPTER SEVENTY-ONE

Late summer I met Sister Lucinda Whiticker, a nun, from St. George Catholic Church. The meeting was completely coincidental. I had walked up to Jenkins Hospital to visit Hazel who was recovering from an appendectomy. I was combing her long brown hair and twisting it into a bun when Sister Lucinda walked in the door.

Hazel had recently been attending the St. George Catholic Church and had become acquainted with Sister Lucinda. Hazel introduced us, and a friendship quickly sparked. Hazel told her about me working for her when I was a teenager and about my recent loss. Sister Lucinda asked me if I was looking for a job. I excitedly exclaimed, "Yes!"

She explained that the Order of Sisters from St. George ran the hospital, and they were in need of a Nurse's Aide.

Hazel smiled at Sister Lucinda, "Lucy would be a perfect fit. I have never met anyone with any more compassion and love, and she is always looking for someone to help."

Sister Lucinda looked back at me, "It sounds like you come with a high recommendation. Can you fill out an application, and plan on starting work next week?"

Hastily, I replied, "That's perfect! My kids start to school on Monday, and that will give me time to find someone to keep Sue."

I could not believe my luck. I was just paying Hazel Painter a visit, and, in turn, I got myself a job.

I filled out my application that night and returned it to Sister Lucinda the following day. She asked me all kinds of questions about Alexander, his tragic death, and my kids. I was chomping at the bit to ask her, "Why on earth would you ever want to be a nun and leave behind the hope of ever having a family of your own?"

I decided that would not be very smart and to just save that question for another day because I did not want to jeopardize this job.

Following the interview, Sister Lucinda sent me for a TB test and told me if my results were negative I should report to work the following Wednesday. She issued me two uniforms and told me that I would need to buy my own white nursing shoes that could be purchased at White's Supply and Uniform for the price of five dollars. She pushed a five dollar bill across her desk in my direction, "Here is an advance on your pay. I will deduct one dollar a week for your first five weeks."

She gave me a wink and smile. I graciously bowed my head toward her and said, "Thank you so much, and I promise you won't be sorry for giving me this opportunity."

I knew the timing must be right because the very next day Bonnie told me about her neighbor, Connie, whose niece had recently come to Jenkins and was looking for work. The following day I met Connie's niece, Maizy Miller. With blue eyes, dark skin, and coal black hair Maizy was a beauty. She was nineteen years old and had come to Kentucky at the insistence of her father. Her mother struggled with alcoholism and was encouraging Maizy to take to the bottle too. Her father did not want her to follow in her mom's footsteps and felt her Aunt Connie would be a much better role model for her.

Maizy proved to be a very well-mannered young lady who readily admitted to loving children and wanted to work. I decided to give her a chance and hired her on to take care of Sue and the boys while I worked. Everything just seemed to be falling into place, and I felt my life was finally getting back on track.

CHAPTER SEVENTY-TWO

I started work on September 13, 1950. This was my first real job, and I was now making one dollar per hour. I could hardly believe that come Friday I would be getting my first ever paycheck, paid in real money, not script. I was so excited to be supporting my family.

My first day consisted of reading a booklet about patient care and watching a short film discussing nurse-aide duties. I shadowed another nurse's aide for the next two days. I felt very comfortable in this environment because I had been taking care of babies and sick folk since I was eight years old.

As I was leaving on Friday afternoon, Sister Lucinda handed me my check and patted my shoulder. I smiled and thanked her for this wonderful opportunity. I walked down the sidewalk holding my paycheck tight in my hand. I crossed the street and made my way to the First National Bank. I walked inside and carefully opened the envelope to reveal a check made out to Lucy Hornaday for the amount of twenty dollars and eighty-two cents. I took a seat and waited for my turn. In a few short minutes, I was leaving the bank with the cash inside my envelope.

When I arrived home, Maizy was in the sitting room playing with Sue, while the boys played out in the yard. I paid Maizy the amount we had agreed on, and she returned to her Aunt Connie's for the weekend.

I decided, instead of cooking supper, I would take all the kids to the recreation center and treat them to hot dogs. This was the first time I had taken the kids on an outing by myself since Alexander died. The boys spotted a couple of their school friends as we walked into the center, and they ran over to talk to them. I carried Sue to the closest table, and we sat down. Ms. Meade spotted Sue and me and came over to chat. We made small talk for a few minutes while she folded a paper napkin over and over until it was the size of a quarter. Then out of nowhere she just blurted out, "Lucy, I don't think you know this, but my daddy got killed in a car wreck when I was about Joe's age, and if I could give you one piece of advice it would be to stay in touch with Alexander's side of the family. My momma never did, and I have always held a grudge against her for not keeping us connected to Daddy's side. I think it made me miss Daddy even more losing all those connections to him."

Just as she began unfolding that same paper napkin the boys ran over and Alfred announced, "Momma, I'm starved."

I thanked Ms. Meade for her advice and told her I needed to get my kids a hot dog.

I sat at that table eating hotdogs with my kids, while listening to them talk and giggle. I began daydreaming about Alexander and our first meeting at this Recreation Center, and how some twelve years later, here I sit with our four kids.

I knew Ms. Meade was right. I did need to keep my children connected to Alexander's side of the family, even if I did hold some resentment and hard feelings against them for attempting to take away my babies. I knew the only way to work through the feelings was to write both of his brothers a letter asking for them to remain a part of their three nephews and niece's life.

That very night, after I tucked all my babies into bed, I put my pen to paper and wrote letters to both of Alexander's brothers. I informed them of my intent to keep my children, but at the same time wanting them to remain a part of their lives. I felt better after writing those letters and getting them ready to mail.

I knew God must have intentionally put Ms. Meade in my path because that conversation helped me realize how my children needed that connection to their daddy. By writing those letters, it helped me work through the bitterness I felt toward them. I thought to myself, life may throw you lemons once in a while, but if you keep your trust in the Good Lord, He will always help you squeeze out some lemonade.

CHAPTER SEVENTY-THREE

I loved my job at Jenkins Hospital, and the time just seemed to fly. By late winter, Maizy had moved in with us, as I had been asked to work the graveyard shift. I was fine with the change in shifts because I could get my kids off to school every morning and be there for them when they returned home in the evening. It did not take long to learn that the hospital became a much more exciting place after midnight. To tell the truth, there was never a dull moment. It seemed that most babies in Jenkins preferred making their grand debut in the wee hours of the morning, as was the case of Anchel Hornsby.

I will never forget the night that Lester brought Anchel to the hospital in labor with their first baby. Lester was jumping around like a cat on a hot tin roof, and Anchel was rocking back and forth, moaning and groaning, like she was just about to die. The doctor got her into the delivery room, and I went in to help get her situated. As I was helping to get her prepped for delivery, Lester came charging into the room against doctor's orders. When he turned and saw Anchel laying there with her long red hair splayed out across the pillow, he turned completely gray and his legs buckled beneath him as he crumpled to the floor. I ran and got some smelling salts while two nurses dragged him from the room. By the time Lester regained full consciousness, he was the proud papa of a brand new baby boy.

Helping to deliver those babies was the best part of my job. I loved seeing the expression on each mother's face as she saw her new baby for the first time. Almost all those new mothers had the look of pure love and admiration in their eyes upon seeing her baby, but on a few occasions, I did witness a look of shock on the mother's face like I know I did not just give birth to that! Even for those shocking deliveries, I must say, it was not long before those mothers, too, viewed their new creation to be the beautiful miracle that it was intended.

Over the next several months I developed a very warm relationship with Sister Lucinda. After I had been working at the hospital for a year, she invited me to visit her and the Sisters at the Parish House. The Parish House was located behind the hospital in close proximity to the lake. In fact, that little community was referred to as Lakeside. Sister Lucinda invited me on a Saturday evening and asked that I bring Sue with me. I dressed Sue in her pretty white dress with a pink satin bow tied at the waist, and I dressed in my best store bought paisley print blue dress that Alexander bought me for my last birthday that he was alive.

I gave Maizy enough money to take the boys to the recreation center and buy them all hot dogs and drinks. By the time I finished getting everyone cleaned up and out of the house, it was already getting dark.

Sue and I began our trek up the long hill toward Lakeside. I had Sue by the hand as we began climbing the steps that led up to the Parish House. When we finally made it to the top of the steps, I reached out to knock on the door causing Sue to lose her balance. Before I could grab her hand, I watched as she fell though the slat on the steps and into what looked to be a culvert. I just knew it was a pipe leading to the lake, and my baby was about to drown. I could not swim a lick myself, but I had to make all attempts to save my baby, so into the "culvert" I, too, jumped.

In under two seconds, I realized Sue and I were trapped inside a coal bin. It was dark as pitch, Sue was crying, and I was trying to console her while attempting to find a way out of this bin without anyone seeing us. I must have worked for the better part of an hour to get us out. When we emerged, we both looked like we had pulled a double shift in the dustiest coal mine in all of Kentucky. I did not even attempt to wipe us off. I just picked Sue up and carried her the mile back home.

When we walked in the door Maizy's mouth dropped open, "What on earth happened to you?"

I told her about our ordeal, and she laughed so hard she developed hiccups that lasted way into the night.

When I finally got Sue and myself cleaned up, I made a declaration to myself and everyone else within ear shot that I would never take another trip after dark.

CHAPTER SEVENTY-FOUR

I n early fall of 1951, I received a letter from Bessie, informing me that she was going to have another baby. I was so happy because after birthing Timmy who proved a difficult delivery, and having had a miscarriage two years later, I was afraid she had decided not to try that again. Immediately after reading her letter, I wrote back and told her how happy I was to get the news, and that I was already praying for a girl.

In a few weeks, Bessie wrote back and told me that she was doing fine, and the doctor said she should deliver in early March. I felt a twinge of pain race through my stomach when I read this. I was not what you call superstitious because I was not afraid of walking under a ladder or having someone sweep under my feet, but March had proved to be a bad luck month for me. I decided not to entertain that bad thought, instead, focus on the new addition to the Elmore clan.

Bessie sent another letter after Christmas in which she stated:

"Sis, I think I am going to have twins. I have gained so much weight, and there is constant movement in my stomach. I never

remember Timmy moving around this much. I can hardly sleep at night, and the kicking circles my entire stomach. I know one thing, if I'm not carrying twins, this baby will definitely be an Olympian because he/she can move all around my stomach in record time."

I laughed out loud while reading Bessie's letter. I could not help but think back to my pregnant days and how much I loved to feel my babies kicking inside me. It did not seem possible that my youngest was already four years old.

On March 14th 1952 I received word by Daddy that Bessie had given birth to identical twin girls, but only one survived. I gave thought to the idea that March was the reason for this misfortune, but I knew in my heart that was not the case. It was a mere coincidence.

I talked to Bessie two days later and told her how I wished I could be there with her.

She responded, "Lucy, I'm fine. I told myself I would not grieve over the one I lost because I still have one that God left in my care. Did Daddy tell you her name, Lucy?"

"No, Bessie, he just told me you had a girl."

"I named her Grace because it was by the grace of God that she survived."

"Oh Bessie, that is such a beautiful name with the most wonderful story that she can carry with her always."

There was a moment of silence, and I heard Bessie let out a sigh before speaking, "We buried our baby girl at Roaring River Baptist Church beside our other baby."

I did not respond; the moment was too bittersweet.

After a long pause Bessie's words quivered from her mouth, "I guess Momma's rocking one of my babies while I rock the other one."

I closed my eyes and replied, "And she is loving every minute of it."

When I hung up the phone, I prayed for God to give Bessie peace and understanding.

That night, when I tucked my babies in bed, I hugged them a little tighter and thanked God for His continued mercy on me and my kids.

CHAPTER SEVENTY-FIVE

Following Bessie's loss, things seemed to calm down, and the next year seemed to be moving along pretty smoothly with very few bumps in the road.

In the fall of 1954, Joe entered high school. I had taken notice that Joe was not my baby any longer but was now coming into his own. He had taken on a paper route, and I soon realized he had his daddy's work ethic. Every morning he folded and bound those newspapers just so and made sure that every one of them was delivered on time and in the same exact location each day. He even took on an extra job washing cars on Saturdays to make his own spending money. He had proved himself reliable and trustworthy, and I could depend on Joe to do what was asked of him.

It was that fall that I bought Maizy a bus ticket to Bluefield, West Virginia to be close to her brother, sister-in-law, and new nephew. I hated to let Maizy go, but I came home from work one morning to find a hole that she burned in Sue's pajamas from one of her cigarettes. I explained to her that I just could not risk her burning up one of my babies. We all cried as we watched Maizy board the bus. Apart from this one incident, Maizy had been a perfect fit for our family.

Immediately, I began to look for Maizy's replacement. I had to have someone that could look after my kids so I could continue working. I spread the word around that I was in need of a hired girl. It was no time until I was introduced to Betty Toliver. She was a pretty, thin, blonde with flawless porcelain skin from East Jenkins, who exuded self-confidence. She quickly informed me that she was eighteen and very mature for her age. She explained that she needed a job and loved babies. I informed her that my babies were no longer babies but ranged in age from six to nearly fifteen. She said that she was up to the task, so I decided to hire her on a trial basis and see how things went.

She met my kids that very afternoon upon their return from school. Norman, Alfred, and Sue were not overly zealous as they had grown attached to Maizy, but Sue did comment, "Boy, you sure are pretty."

It was not long until I saw Joe walking up over the hill. I introduced Betty as our new hired girl, and I watched as Joe's eyes lit up and nearly popped out of his head. He scurried off to his room and returned moments later with his hair slicked back and sporting enough cologne to peel the wallpaper off the walls. He briskly walked past Betty and me and continued on out the door. I got a suspicion that this arrangement may not be the best, but I needed this to work until I had other options.

After Betty left, I rounded up the kids for supper. I asked what they thought of the new hired girl. Norman and Alfred mumbled something about wanting Maizy back, but Joe looked straight at me and said, "Mom, do you want my honest opinion?"

I replied, "Certainly."

I could not wait to hear what was going on inside that head of his.

"I think she is perfect, and since I am already in high school, I could stay up late and show her all the ropes."

My eyes widened and I felt all my facial muscles tense. I tried to soften my look as I replied," I appreciate that, Honey, but you need your sleep. I will tell her all she needs to know before I go to work."

He smiled, "Well, just let me know what I can do; after all, I am almost fifteen."

I knew right then that this arrangement could not work long term, and I had to come up with another plan.

Two weeks later, I had a new job working at Robo's Dairy Bar. Sister Lucinda begged me to stay on at the hospital, but I told her my kids had to come first. I would have work hours that would coincide with the school day, and I could be home with my kids at night.

I was really excited about my new job. I had always enjoyed cooking meals and on occasion delivering my home cooking to the sick and shut-ins. I must confess that I enjoyed cooking almost as much as I loved taking care of sick folk.

I could not wait to get my children off to school the morning I began my new job. On my way to the Drive-In, I could envision all the hungry men lined up to get short orders prepared by me. All too quickly, I found out that cooking for the public is not as easy as cooking for four kids.

Around twelve o'clock, lines began forming outside the two windows, and they grew longer and longer. The lead server, Nadine, told me to help take orders at her window and watch her preparation routine before working my own window. I began helping to take orders, all the while watching her routine as she prepared a burger, then a hotdog, followed by fries and a banana split. I could feel myself growing more and more nervous. In short time, Nadine looked over and said, "I think you are ready to work your own window now."

I walked over and opened my window announcing, "Can I help you, sir?"

A tall, slender man with the name, "Hobart," sewed to the pocket of his brown work uniform lowered his head into the window, "I would like a hot dog all the way."

I walked over and got a bun, but seeing the never ending line form outside my window made me dizzy, and my mind just went blank. I walked back to my window carrying my bun, as I blurted out, "Now, what does this need?"

Hobart laughed, "Well, a weenie for one thing."

I got tickled, and as I began laughing, I felt the tension ease from my body. The rest of my shift seemed little more than a blur. By the time I had served the last customer, I felt like I had pulled a double shift….no, a triple shift… at the hospital.

That afternoon, as I walked home, I could feel a smile creeping across my face as I whispered under my breath, "Lucy, feeding hungry men is not all you had it cracked up to be."

CHAPTER SEVENTY-SIX

The remainder of that year proved to be an interesting one. That winter was bitter cold and the first one I had spent without a hired girl since Alexander died. It was by God's grace and mercy that we did not freeze to death that winter.

The kids knew how scared of fire I had been my entire life. I hated the idea of having to build a fire in our Warm Morning Stove to heat our house. With no other adult around to ease my fears, every morning and evening faced with that task was pure torture. I panicked to see the stovepipe glow red, indicating the fire was hot enough to emit heat throughout the house. On those few occasions that the pipe did glow, I put on a show for the kids whooping and hollering while running for the fire extinguisher that Alexander had bought so many years before. I would sit on the couch with the extinguisher pointed toward the stove until the glow would start to fade. The kids would amusingly watch, as I did my "fire dance", as Alfred called it.

I worked hard to keep the fire from getting too hot and tried my best to keep it just a notch above a smolder. To manage the fire,

I used my kids as the litmus test. In the early mornings and late evenings, they would all gather around the stove and hold their socked feet to the pipe. When their feet dropped to the floor, I knew it was time to quit adding coal.

As cold as that winter proved to be inside our house, as well as outside, not one of us got sick, not even so much as a cold. Joe commented sometime later it was because germs could not grow in a subzero environment. Whatever the case, we bundled in layers of clothing and went to bed under mountains of quilts. We awoke many mornings to find our goldfish frozen in its bowl. I even re-member on one occasion, washing my work clothes and hanging them up in the sitting room, only to find them in a stiff, frozen state the following morning.

What sticks out most in my mind from the winter of '54 are the times all of us snuggled on the couch under a quilt, eating my homemade chocolate candy, and telling stories. I knew these days were fleeting, as Joe was almost grown, and my other two boys were not far behind. Our house may have been cold as ice that winter, but our home was always a very warm place to be.

CHAPTER SEVENTY-SEVEN

I worked at Robo's for several months, and I found the work to be more tiring than my work at the hospital. The onset of the brand new school year also brought about job openings within the school system, one of which was an opening for a cafeteria worker at Jenkins Independent School. I decided to apply, as I would be on the same schedule as my kids. I had decided that feeding hungry kids could never be as tiring as feeding all those hungry men that frequented Robo's.

Once again, I could not believe my luck. I was offered the job the same day I applied. I jumped at the opportunity and gave my notice at Robo's the following day. Nadine seemed surprised that I was leaving. She walked over and stood beside me as I was cleaning up after the lunch rush. She was chomping on a piece of gum and popping it between her teeth while she talked, "I don't know why you are quitting; you are a natural at this."

I smiled at Nadine but gave no response.

She let out a long sigh, "I dread having to train the next one. It seems you get at least three bad ones for every good one, and the good ones just don't stay that long."

I began to sing *"My trains off the track, and I can't get it back"* and Nadine joined in singing and popping her gum in perfect time.

That particular day we left work together, as she offered me a ride home. As she was pulling up onto B&O Hill, she said, "Why don't you get yourself a car, Lucy? Sure would make things easier for you."

I smiled, "Don't really have a need for one, besides I don't even have a license."

Nadine got this wild look in her eye, "I have an idea. I'll get my brother to teach you to drive, and then you can get your license. Besides, Joe will soon be sixteen, and you know that he will be chomping at the bit to drive."

I knew Nadine had an ulterior motive. She had tried for months to set me up with her brother, and I knew she was making one last ditch attempt to get us together. I told her that I would think about it and let her know what I decided.

As I opened the door to get out, Nadine said, "He's got a brand new '55 Ford Thunderbird and you sure would look good driving it."

I smiled and thanked her for the ride home.

I thought about my conversation with Nadine all evening. It really would be nice to learn to drive and having a car would render me so much more independence. Even though I was not interested in a relationship with Nadine's brother, I decided to take Nadine up on her offer if her brother was indeed willing to teach me how to drive.

The following Saturday I was getting my first driving lesson in Frank Collins' new Thunderbird. Nadine had forewarned me that Frank was a talker, but my goodness, I never dreamed anyone could possibly talk in one continuous sentence without ever stopping to take in a full breath. As soon as I got in and closed the door, Frank's mouth started up. He did not make small talk or ask questions about me and the kids, he talked cars. He told me all about the mechanics of a car, how it should be taken care of and driven, and how much the parts would cost if "heaven forbid" I should wreck it. By the time we got to Peak's Branch, the site for my first driving lesson, I was a nervous wreck. I could just see myself getting the brake and the gas mixed up and running that brand new car in a ditch. He had been informing me the whole way here how expensive the replacement parts were, and I knew it would be next to impossible for me to save enough money to replace even as much as the side mirror.

Frank told me to take my position in the driver's seat while he went around to the passenger's side. He scooted over to the middle of the seat. I must have given him the evil eye because he held up both hands and said, "Don't worry, I'm just sitting here to help out should something go wrong."

Frank did not say another word as I put my foot on the brake and shifted the car into drive. I could not believe it, Frank was not talking, but sat holding his breath as I placed both hands firmly on the steering wheel and softly tapped the gas. I would tap the gas and let off, then tap again and let off. We were sort of hopping down Peak's Branch when Frank again began to speak, "You are going to flood this car driving like this. You need to keep steady pressure on the gas pedal, but not too much."

I did what he said, and we made the six mile drive down Peak's Branch and back in just under an hour. I never let the speed get above ten miles per hour for fear that I might forget how to use the brake. I know Frank was relieved after my first lesson because once he took position back in the driver's seat he again went to talking and did not shut up until he let me out back home.

Frank came to the house every Saturday for the next five weeks, and I would have a driving lesson. I began to feel more comfortable behind the wheel, and I know Frank began to feel more comfortable with my driving because he wasn't doing all that nervous talking anymore. That last Saturday that Frank took me driving he asked if he could join me and the kids at church the next day.

I replied, "You are welcome to come to Wright's Holler Freewill Baptist Church anytime, but I'm not ready for another man in my life. I have my kids to think about, and I reckon they take about all my time."

Frank immediately dropped the subject and said he would be back the following week to take me to Whitesburg to get my license.

As I was getting out of the car that day I reached over and patted Frank on the arm, "You are a good friend Frank, and I really do thank you for teaching me to drive."

The following Friday, Frank and I made the trip to Whitesburg, and I took the driving test in Frank's new Thunderbird. That proved to be a blessing in disguise because the licensing examiner was much more interested in Frank's car than my driving. He rubbed on the dashboard and sat admiring all the shiny knobs and chrome and paid little attention to my driving ability.

I left Whitesburg that day with my very own driver's license. I was amazed at how much this one little card boosted my confidence level. I thought, I may not have a high school diploma, but I have a license to drive a car, and now the whole world is my oyster.

CHAPTER SEVENTY-EIGHT

The following spring I purchased my very first car. Mrs. Sebastian, one of my neighbors from the top of the holler, knew that I had recently gotten my driver's license and asked if I was interested in buying her 1950 Nash Rambler, as she was in the market for a new car. I decided to have a look at the car and took Joe with me. I knew that he would be interested because he was already sixteen and was ready to start driving himself.

Joe thought the car was perfect for us, and I really could not see anything wrong with it myself other than the color. It was yellow, and I would have preferred red, but the price was right, so I decided to buy it.

The next day we took care of all the legalities, and I took ownership of the Nash Rambler. All the kids were excited when I came driving down the hill in our newly purchased car. I pulled into the driveway where they all piled in and we headed out for a joy ride. Alfred and Norman immediately wanted me to "put the pedal to the metal" as they called it.

I laughed, pushed the pedal to the floor and quickly released the pedal, causing it to backfire. The loud boom caused us to nearly jump out of our skins. I chuckled, "Well, we won't try that again because we just might blow up."

I looked in my rear view mirror to see Alfred, Norman, and Sue sliding across the back seat giggling and laughing. Joe, who was sitting in the front seat with me, was eyeing all the gauges and knobs along the dashboard. As Norman, Alfred, and Sue talked and giggled, Joe held this serious look on his face. I knew the wheels in his brain were turning. I glanced over, "What are you thinking, Joe?"

"Well, I was thinking maybe you could teach me to drive, since we have this car, and since I'm already sixteen I could get my driver's license to help you out with all the driving."

I winked, "We'll see."

The very next week I was at Peak's Branch giving Joe a driving lesson. I took in a deep breath as Joe walked around the car to take the driver's seat while I scooted to the passenger's side. Once Joe got in and shut the door, I slid back to the middle of the seat until I was practically behind the steering wheel, too. Joe placed his hands on the wheel and looked over at me, "Mom, do you mind scooting over, you are practically in my lap."

I scooted over a few inches, as Joe shifted the gear into drive and accelerated. He did not gingerly tap the gas as I had during my first lesson; he held increasingly steady pressure to the pedal as we began gaining speed. I began whooping and stomping the floorboard like it was a brake. Joe looked over, "What's wrong?"

I replied, "You're going a little too fast for my liking."

He rolled his eyes, "We are only going thirty."

I snapped, "Well, I think you should hold it to ten until you get the feel for it."

Joe didn't say another word; he just lifted his foot from the gas pedal as the car began to decelerate. Joe seemed completely comfortable behind the wheel, and by the end of the month he, too, had a driver's license. He came out of the examiner's office holding up that license with a grin spread across his entire face.

I knew how much more independent I felt the day I left the licensing examiner with that license in my hand. I sensed that Joe was experiencing those same feelings. I knew in my heart that Joe was at the threshold of becoming a man, but in my eyes he would always be my baby.

CHAPTER SEVENTY-NINE

Once Joe got his license to drive, our Nash Rambler never had a minute's peace. Joe seemed to forget that he had walked to the store, movies, and school ballgames for years. He was continually asking to drive the car to all those locations previously within walking distance. I gave in to his desires and allowed him the driving practice. I would always forewarn him that I was watching and also had my spies planted throughout town, and if it got back to me that he was driving recklessly he would have to resort to walking again. I knew how level- headed Joe had always been, and I wanted to see if the power of a car would render him weak.

Joe proved to be as trustworthy and level-headed behind the wheel as he was in other situations.

It seemed that once Joe went to driving, my boys were no longer tied to my coat-tail. It was not long before Joe took an interest in girls, and our car spent most Saturday nights down in Seco, while Joe courted Joyce Miller. His sudden interest in girls seemed to rub off on Alfred- Norman was born interested in girls- just one of many reasons that I needed those eyes in the back of my head. I was beginning to see that parenting teenagers was more of a challenge than I had ever realized.

Working in the school cafeteria was my only saving grace, as it allowed me the opportunity to keep close tabs on my boys.

Soon after Joe began dating, Alfred, too, took notice of a young girl from Burdine named Irene Goforth. I could tell that Alfred was really smitten with her. Where Joe seemed more casually interested in Joyce, Alfred had definitely been bitten by the love bug.

Irene was a mere child, but Alfred had fallen hard for her. I guess it was her long, blonde curls, blue eyes, and Barbie doll looks that hooked him, and I knew there was no talking him out of it. It was during times like this that I longed for Alexander because I knew my boys needed that male role model in their life.

It was not long before Joe was driving Alfred to Burdine on an almost weekly basis to court Irene. I knew Irene's parents. They were a highly respected, hardworking, God-fearing family. I also knew better than to meddle too much when it came to matters of the heart. Experience had taught me that meddling would only make the attraction stronger.

In a blink of an eye, Alfred, too, had his license, and then our little Rambler never had time to cool its engine. Once Alfred was comfortable behind the wheel our car spent more time in Irene's driveway than ours.

I wanted Alfred to enjoy his teenage years and not tie himself down to a girl when they were both so young. At the same time, I knew Alfred was completely wrapped around Irene's little finger. I could only pray that he would finish school before any wedding bells were rung.

CHAPTER EIGHTY

A s the old saying goes, time waits for no one, and in late spring of 1958 my first born graduated from Jenkins Independent School. I could never express in words how proud I was as Joe walked across the stage and accepted his diploma. He had completed 12 years of school, having only missed one day total, in those twelve years. He had accomplished the goal I so wanted to achieve so many years prior, and I was overcome with emotion knowing that he had completed this wonderful feat. I knew I could have never raised him to adulthood without the help of the Good Lord, and I had to give Him all of the credit for His blessings and guidance during these last eighteen years.

I expressed to Joe and my other two boys early on that I did not want to give any one of them up to the Kentucky coal mines, like I had their daddy. I wanted them to spread their wings and venture beyond this coal mining town, but I had not given real thought to what I had been wishing for until I was sent word late summer after Joe's graduation that he had joined the Army and was on his way to Columbia, South Carolina for basic training. The army recruiter that gave me that shocking news informed me that Joe would not be allowed to call home until the following week.

I could not believe that he had left without as much as a good-bye. I felt all panicky inside thinking of my baby enlisting in the armed services. He would be carrying and using a gun for Pete's sake (the one item I forbade from my house.)

The week of Joe's anticipated phone call I did not venture far from the house. We were still on summer break, and I had not yet returned to work. I received that highly anticipated phone call on Thursday afternoon, and when I heard his voice I felt the tears welling up in my eyes. I knew Joe was a little shaken, too, because he hesitated before clearing his throat to speak.

"Momma, I guess you've heard I joined the Army."

I could not hold back my tears. "Are you all right? Do you have enough to eat?"

"I'm fine Momma. George came with me on the buddy plan, and we will be together the whole time. Don't worry, Momma, the food is good, and I have plenty to eat."

I wiped the tears from my eyes, "What on earth possessed you to join the Army, Joe?"

"You always said you didn't want me to work in the mines, and I saw this as an opportunity to see the world and earn money to someday go on to college. I'll be making more money than I ever made in my life, and I intend to send some of it home, so you won't have to work so hard."

I knew I had to swallow this bitter pill; after all, I had discouraged him from working the mines and never wanted my boys tied to Jenkins the rest of their lives.

"Joe, remember this, *"It's a great life if you don't weaken, but who wants to be strong.'"*

"What do you mean, Momma?"

"Well, it's sort of like a riddle. From my earliest memories, I remember my momma using that quote from time to time when something profound had just happened, or she was anticipating something to happen."

"Momma, the riddle, what do you think it means for me?"

"I will tell you that the quote has spoken to me since I was a little girl. As I have matured and grown, its meaning has grown and changed. Over time you, too, will figure out what it means for you. Just remember your momma loves you. Make sure you write home every week, and I will answer all your letters."

Thanks, Momma. I love you."

"I love you too, Sugar."

"Bye, Momma."

"Joe, you remember, "*It's a great life if you don't weaken, but who wants to be strong.*""

CHAPTER EIGHTY-ONE

Joe's leaving home brought Momma's quote forefront in my mind again. I had not thought a lot about the quote since Alexander's death, and I knew it was speaking to me for some unknown reason. Just like Momma, the quote seemed to speak to me during times of change.

That night, after Joe's phone call, as I was combing my hair, I looked at myself in the mirror. I could not believe that a middle aged woman was staring back at me. Where did all the time go? I had been so busy raising my kids since Alexander's death that I had not given much thought to what my life would be like after my last one left home.

My heart ached for Joe, and I knew this was just the beginning. If the feelings between Alfred and Irene did not change, I knew Alfred, too, would be leaving soon.

I crawled into bed that night and grabbed my Bible from the night stand. I opened it up to the Psalm that still sheltered my precious clover. I reached down to gently touch it, as Sue crawled in bed beside me. She looked over and said, "Mom, did you find that four leaf clover?"

I replied, "Yes, do you want to hear the story?"

"Yes! Will you tell it to me?"

I placed the Bible back on the nightstand, and I snuggled down under the covers with Sue scooched up against me. I told her the story about the day I found the clover, the wish I made, and how I had cherished that clover all these years. After I finished the story, Sue turned her head and looked at me, "Mom, I'm sure glad God sent me to you and not to someone else."

I kissed her forehead, "Me, too, Sue, me, too."

I lay there that night looking at Sue, listening to the muffled voices of Alfred and Norman in the next room, and thinking of Joe some four hundred miles away. I felt a tear burning in the corner of my eye as I softly whispered, "*It's a great life if you don't weaken, but who wants to be strong.*"

CHAPTER EIGHTY-TWO

Once the new school year started I was ready to return to my cafeteria duties at the school. Getting back to work provided a distraction and gave me less time to sit and worry about Joe. I had already received two letters from him and, from reading between the lines, I could tell he was already homesick. I tried to keep my return letters positive and light. I did not want him to regret his decision; after all, the Army now owned him for at least the next three years.

At the same time, Alfred's interest in Irene was not waning, and the fire between them seemed to intensify. I knew they were planning their future because I had overheard some of their conversations that began with "after we get married." This was Alfred's last year of school, and I was hoping he could make it to graduation before doing anything as rash as putting a wedding band on Irene's finger.

I made a vow with myself to enjoy what time remained before all my kids were grown and out the door and not worry so much about what I would do with myself after they were all gone.

While working in the school cafeteria, I had developed a close friendship with Christine Ball, the cafeteria manager, and Iris Hunt, a co-worker. From time to time, we would meet on Saturday mornings and shop. Christine and Iris both loved to shop. When I say loved, I mean they scoured every rack of clothing, trying on dress after dress, blouse after blouse, and sweater after sweater. I usually just went along for the trip because I had no extra money to buy myself anything, but I would stand outside the dressing room and go fetch what they wanted to try on next, so they did not have to dress and undress so many times.

It was on one of these shopping trips in early fall that I spied a beautiful A-line button through crimson red dress, with the most beautiful mother of pearl buttons. The dress caught my eye because it was hanging on a mannequin in the window of Danson's Dress Shop. I commented on the dress, and Christine insisted that I try it on.

I carried the dress into the dressing room and put in on, admiring each button down the front of the dress as I twisted it though the button eye. I walked outside the dressing room and twirled around, admiring myself in the three-sided mirror.

Christine and Iris both commented at the same time, "You need to buy that Lucy; it has your name written all over it."

I looked down at the price tag- $8.58.

"I can't possibly buy this dress. Where in the world would I find $ 8.58!"

I wrinkled up my nose, "You know my money tree dried up and has refused to bloom for the last several years."

Christine smiled a mischievous smile before responding, "I'll make a deal with you, Lucy. If you can get me a date with Jim Mann, I will personally buy you the dress."

I was floored, "You mean Paula's widower, Jim?"

"That's the one!"

"You want a date with Jim Mann for this red dress?"

"Yes!"

I twirled around again in front of the three way mirror, admiring the dress once more before announcing, "You've got yourself a deal!"

I was not sure how I was going to go about getting Christine her date, but I left Danson's Dress shop that day confident that the beautiful red dress would soon be hanging in my closet.

CHAPTER EIGHTY-THREE

I had never played matchmaker before, but I knew I would not stop short of getting Jim and Christine out on a date because a new red dress was on the line.

I knew Jim from year's past. I had helped to take care of his wife, Paula, when I worked at the hospital. Paula had cancer and spent her last weeks in Jenkins Hospital. Since she and Jim had no children or other family living nearby, Jim was left all alone with the arduous task of tending to Paula. Jim had asked if I would keep a close check on her while he worked. I agreed to take on this added responsibility, and during this time Jim and I developed a friendship. In fact, I was sitting with Paula, holding her hand, when she passed that Friday evening some eight years ago.

I would occasionally see Jim when I made a trip into town. He was always alone and, to my knowledge, had never dated since Paula's death. I suspected that, just like me, he was not interested in another relationship, which could put my new red dress in jeopardy.

I knew he ate most of his evening meals at Bogg's Lunch Counter. I decided to make a trip to Bogg's on Wednesday evening for supper. Bogg's featured chicken and dumplings on Wednesday's, and I had been told they were the best in town. I knew Jim loved chicken and dumplings from my time spent with Paula, and I figured he would definitely be there then.

After school on Wednesday evening, I told Sue we were going to Bogg's to eat chicken and dumplings. Sue responded, "Why don't we go to the Recreation Center and eat a hot dog because we can eat chicken and dumplings here at home anytime."

I told Sue that this wasn't about the chicken and dumplings but about a new dress and for her to just accompany me and keep her mouth in check.

I had Alfred drive us down to Bogg's and let us out before he and Norman drove over to the Recreation Center to eat. When Sue and I walked into the door, I saw Jim sitting at the lunch counter, with a heaping plate of chicken and dumplings before him. There were several stools empty alongside Jim, and I walked over and sat on the stool beside him with Sue sitting beside me.

I felt a little nervous and jittery inside because I did not know how I was going to approach the topic of Christine.

When the waitress walked over, I told her we would have one order of chicken and dumplings with an extra plate. Jim recognized my voice and glanced over at me.

"Miss Lucy, it has been a long time since I saw you. What brings you here?"

"Well, I keep hearing everyone rave about these chicken and dumplings, and I decided to find out for myself if they are all that."

For a few minutes we made small talk while I worked up my nerve. I noticed that Jim was getting down to his last few bites of dumplings, and I knew I had to bring up Christine. I wiped my mouth with my napkin, before turning my head in Jim's direction.

"Jim, do you know Christine.....ah, Christine Ball?"

"You mean Paul Ball's widow?"

I exclaimed, "Yes! That's her."

"I remember Paul very well, but I am not acquainted with his widow."

"Well, Jim, this is your lucky day because Christine wants to meet you. How would you like a date with her?"

Jim looked me dead in the eye and his response was not at all what I expected, "Miss Lucy, there is only one woman in this town that I would date, and only one woman that I would marry, and I'm looking at her right now."

To say I was a little taken back was an understatement. I began to stammer before blurting out, "Please just take her on one date because a red dress is on the line."

"What did you say?"

I immediately began spilling the beans, "Christine promised me a new red dress if I could get her a date with you. Please, just one date, and if you don't like her you're off the hook, but it will mean a new red dress for me."

Jim smiled, "Well, I guess I could meet Christine. Now, if I'm not interested in her, say…. would you be willing to give me a date?"

I could feel myself getting all flushed, and my stomach began to knot. I did not have a response, especially with Sue now practically in my lap, holding on to every word being spoken. How I wished that I had sent her to the Recreation Center with the boys for that hot dog.

I reached up and tucked my hair behind my ear. "Well, we will see, but first things first."

Before we left Bogg's that evening, we had our game plan ready for Jim's meeting Christine on Saturday night.

When Sue and I got into bed that night she began asking all sorts of questions about Jim and if I was going to marry him. I explained to Sue that she and the boys came first, and I was not

looking to get married again, but if the right opportunity present-
ed itself and she and her brothers were ok with it, I might.

Sue turned her head in my direction and tucked her arms under her pillow. She bit down on her bottom lip as a look of concern
swept across her face, "Momma, what if you do get married again
and he does not like us, does that mean that I will have to leave
home like you did?"

I reached over and cupped half her face in my right hand,
"Sugar, I have no intentions of getting married right now, but there
is one thing for certain, no man will ever come before you, Alfred,
Norman, and Joe."

Sue leaned over and kissed my cheek.

I kissed my palm and touched it to her forehead. "Now, you get
to sleep and have sweet dreams."

I rolled over and closed my eyes, but I could not get the lunch
counter conversation out of my mind. Could it be possible for me
to fall in love again? I had never thought of Jim in this way before,
and I knew he was at least fifteen years my senior.

I had to admit he had conjured up feelings inside me that had
been dead for years, but I would not allow myself to go there yet
because Jim needed to meet Christine first. They could prove a
perfect match. For the time being, I needed to keep that red dress
forefront in my mind.

CHAPTER EIGHTY-FOUR

I could not wait to get to school the next day and inform Christine that I had her date lined up for Saturday. She squealed like a young school girl then begged me for the details of our conversation. I told her that Jim knew her late husband very well and looked forward to getting acquainted with her. She kept hounding me for details, but I was not about to tell her what he really said, and I was not going to make up lies either. I did not want to get her hopes up too high in case they did not prove a perfect match.

Later that afternoon, as I finished cleaning the tables in the cafeteria, Christine walked over and asked if I would come by her house later in the evening to help her pick out the perfect dress for Saturday night. I told her that I would be there around 6:00pm, after I got my kids fed.

Iris was already at Christine's when I arrived, and Iris seemed as excited as Christine about this "date." I sort of felt sick and wanted to tell her that she should keep her emotions in check, but I sorely wanted that red dress, and this "love affair" between Christine and Jim needed to last until that dress was resting in my closet.

I smiled at Christine and said, "If this works out between you and Jim, I am going to apply right away for my matchmaking license. With the many widows and widowers in this town, I should be swamped for business."

I wrinkled my nose and laughed out loud. Iris responded, "Lucy, I can't believe how quickly you got her a date."

I smiled at Iris, "Didn't you know that I can make nine day pickles in ninety minutes. Now let's help Christine find her dating dress."

When Christine opened the door to her closet, it was like opening the door to Danson's Dress Shop. I had never seen so many dresses and outfits in one person's closet. I thought she must spend her entire paycheck on new clothes. After two long hours of trying on dress after dress, Christine decided on a long sleeved mint green and white polka dot dress that fell just below her knee. I told her I thought it was the perfect choice because I knew Jim to be a very conservative, southern gentleman.

The following day Christine could not stop talking about Jim. If I didn't know any better, I would have thought that they were already a couple. She had now convinced herself that Jim was just chomping at the bit to meet her since he had agreed to the date so soon. I just let her do most of the talking, as I did not want to say anything to get her hopes up more. When I left work that Friday evening, I told Christine to make sure she was ready by seven on Saturday, as I would be introducing them then.

When I woke up Saturday morning I immediately thought about Jim, and I felt this crazy tickling twinge race across my stomach. I told myself to put Jim out of my mind and think about my dress. Sometimes it is impossible to get your mind to cooperate because the more I tried not to think about Jim the more I thought about him. In fact, I thought about Jim the whole day.

Jim arrived at my house at 6:45pm sharp just as we had planned. I reminded myself to keep my nerves in check as I answered the door. There stood Jim in a three piece suit, with the pocket hand-kerchief to match his tie. He tipped his hat and said, "Well, Miss Lucy, you look like pure sunshine in that yellow dress."

I blushed, "Well, thank you, Jim, and you sure are dapperly dressed. Why, you and Christine will make a fine looking couple."

Jim retorted, "I agreed to meet her, and that's all."

Jim and I, again, went over our game plan. I would introduce them and then leave, allowing Christine and Jim to decide the rest of their evening together.

I informed Jim that Sue would be accompanying us, as I had no one to watch her, since my boys were at the ballgame. At the ap-pointed time Jim, Sue, and I walked up to Christine's, as she lived in the same holler as me.

Christine must have been standing right behind the door be-cause it immediately opened upon Jim's first knock. When I saw Christine I knew she had been getting ready for this date all day. She had a beauty parlor coiffure that was teased and curled to perfection. She, too, had spent hours on her makeup, as it ap-peared heavy and overly done- from the thick foundation, two shades darker than her skin tone, to the bright green eye shadow that covered her eyelid from the brow to the lash- not to mention, the false eyelashes sitting a row above her own natural lashes that she had obviously applied without the aid of her glasses. Her fin-gernails were painted the brightest red which clashed against her mint green dress. I knew Christine had taken such pains to make an impression on Jim, and an impression she was making, but not the kind for which she had hoped.

I introduced Christine to Jim, and Jim tipped his hat before removing it from his head. They exchanged a handshake, and Christine invited us all in. I sat in a chair in the far corner of the room with Sue sitting in my lap. This allowed Jim and Christine to share the sofa. Jim sat at one end and Christine at the other.

Christine fidgeted with the hemline on her dress, and Jim sat tapping his fingers on his knee.

After several minutes of awkward silence, I stood up with Sue by my side and told Christine that I would see myself out. As I turned to make my way out the door, I saw Jim stand as well while placing his hat back on his head. He looked at Christine, again stuck out his hand, and said, "It was a pleasure meeting you."

Christine stood and looked like she was about to cry.

I made my way out the door, with Jim following closely behind. I did not know what to do, so I just walked back down the holler toward my house holding to Sue's hand and never peering back at Jim.

When I walked up onto the porch I could hear Jim's footsteps approaching. I sent Sue into the house before turning around to face him. "I thought we had our game plan. You were going to meet Christine so I could get the red dress."

Jim looked at me, "I did meet her, and I knew it was going nowhere. I really didn't want to waste any more of her time."

"I wouldn't call a measly fifteen minutes as wasting anyone's time."

"That would have wasted the time I would like to spend getting to know you."

I did not have a response. I looked up at Jim and let out a sigh.

Keeping an arm's length distance from me he said, "Miss Lucy, I would be most honored if you would accompany me to a picture show next Saturday night."

I felt a flurry of emotion. The whole idea of a new relationship and how my kids would take it made my stomach begin to swell with nervous rumbles.

I looked at Jim, "I guess I could go, if Sue can come with me."

Jim chuckled, "I will see you and Sue next Saturday night."

I watched as Jim got into his car and drove out of the holler.

Growing up, I had heard the old wives tale that love shows up when you least expect it. I could now say that was true because I was minding my own business when it again came knocking at my heart's door.

CHAPTER EIGHTY-FIVE

Monday morning rolled around too fast, and I now had the daunting task of facing Christine. When I walked through the door of the cafeteria, Christine looked my way and then turned and walked into the kitchen. I heard Christine say, "Iris, you can tell Lucy to work the lunch line today."

I walked past the kitchen to the coat closet carrying my pocketbook and sweater. Iris followed me inside. Iris repeated, while rolling her eyes, "Christine wants you to work the lunch line."

I sighed, "I know."

I put my pocketbook and sweater away and went on into the kitchen. I could see Christine sitting at a table tallying up the lunch count for the day. I walked out into the lunchroom, but Christine refused to acknowledge my presence. I decided to let sleeping dogs lie right now and turned and walked back into the kitchen. It felt like I spent the entire day walking around on egg shells. I left work that day emotionally exhausted. The rest of the work week was just as exhausting with Christine's continual refusal to speak to me.

Friday evening could not come soon enough. I was ready to have a couple of days free from Christine's drama, and I was really looking forward to my date with Jim on Saturday night. After breakfast on Saturday morning, I told Sue that Jim was taking us to the picture show later that evening. Sue's eyes widen, "You mean we are going on a date?"

"Yes, and I want you to be on your very best behavior."

Sue and I spent the rest of the day getting ready for "our" date. I washed and curled Sue's hair, as well as mine, and Sue insisted that we wear "matching dresses" that she had picked out from our closet. The dress she picked out for me was not my most flattering, but it was about the same shade of pink as the one Sue had picked out for herself, so I just went along with it.

Jim arrived at 6:00pm sharp and was as dapperly dressed as he had been the previous Saturday night. He tipped his hat and said, "Miss Lucy, you sure look pretty in that pink dress."

I smiled, "Sue picked out our dresses."

Sue stood up, "See, we match."

Jim grinned, "Sue, you look as pretty as your momma."

Jim then held out his arm to me, "Are you girls ready for a picture show?"

Sue blurted out, "Yes! You know I have never been courting before."

Jim chuckled.

I took Jim's arm and Sue's hand, and we headed off to the movies.

As we entered the Recreation Center, I thought back to my first date with Alexander in this same movie theater. Here I was again on another "first date,"... what a coincidence. Unlike my first date with Alexander, I was able to concentrate on this picture show, but there was a definite chemistry between Jim and me. Each time our hands touched as we dipped them into the big tub of popcorn, I felt that tickling twinge in my stomach. I could sense by the way

Jim would look over at me that he was feeling it, too. Even though the sparks were flying between us, Jim minded his manners and made no attempts to touch me in an affectionate way.

Following our date, he walked Sue and me up onto the porch and patted Sue on the head. He then tipped his hat to me and said, "I really enjoyed the night, and I didn't feel like it was wasting our time; at least, I know it did not waste mine."

I smiled as he tipped his hat again and turned to make his way to his car.

I spoke up, "Thanks for the movie. I thought the time just flew by. Goodnight, Jim."

Jim opened his car door, "Goodnight, Lucy, and sweet dreams."

Sue and I went inside and straight to our bedroom. Sue hopped into bed, rested her elbows on her pillow, and cupped her chin in her two open palms. I knew she had something on her mind. I got into bed beside her, and she said, "Momma, I like Jim, and I think maybe we should marry him someday."

I smiled at Sue, "Well, let's not put the cart before the horse."

"Can we at least keep courting him? Courting is a lot of fun."

I whispered, "I hope so, Sue."

Even though we did not make plans for a future date, my sixth sense told me that we were destined to be together.

Since Alexander's death, I had never prayed for a new relationship. This night was different. I prayed for God's direction and guidance as I began this brand new chapter in my life.

CHAPTER EIGHTY-SIX

I guess it goes without saying that the red dress never took up residence in my closet. It was never my intent to "steal" Jim from Christine, as she put it, but I knew better than to argue the point. I had learned from my time living with Aunt Pandy and Albert that no matter what I said Christine was going to believe the story she had worked up in her head, and I could talk until I was blue in the face, but it would only be in vain. At least she had not called me a liar to my face like Aunt Pandy did, so I decided the less said the better.

The remainder of the school year proved to be very tough, as Christine continued to cut my work hours. By the end of the school year, my hours had been cut in half, and I was struggling to make ends meet.

My reduced paychecks rendered it impossible for me to purchase the class ring that Alfred so desperately wanted. I was determined that I was going to buy him that ring because he had used restraint and not yet put that gold band on Irene's finger. I

230

cut every corner I could without sacrificing food for my kids, and I just could not come up with the fifty dollars needed for the ring.

I decided to write Daddy a letter and ask him to borrow the fifty dollars until I could find a full-time job, at which time I would pay him back. Two weeks after I mailed my letter, I received a package in the mail. It was wrapped in brown paper, with Daddy's return address written in the top left hand corner. I took in a deep breath and exhaled very slowly before I opened it. I remembered the only other time I had written to Daddy needing him and how he, or should I say Bertha, just poo pooed away Albert's behavior. I slowly dug my fingernail into the corner of the package and began to tear away the brown paper revealing a case of Mars Bars. I knew the box contained candy because the seal had not been broken. I scoured the package for a letter or at least an explanation, but its only contents was the case of candy. I knew that, just like the letter I wrote Daddy when I was living at Aunt Pandy's, Bertha must have intercepted this one, too.

I felt my face flush as the blood began to boil inside me. I tore open the candy case revealing twenty-four Mars Bars. I grabbed one of the bars, ripped it open, and took a bite. What was I to do now? I could ask Jim for the money, but I did not want him to see me as a weak widow who could not properly manage her finances. I decided to leave it in the Lord's hands, and if this ring was to materialize, He would help me find a way.

Later in the evening, when the kids got in from school, I told them, "Your paw paw sent you all a special treat, and it's on the kitchen table."

Sue went running into the kitchen and emerged, beaming with a Mars Bar in hand.

Sue shouted, "How did Paw Paw know that Mars Bars are my favorite?"

I replied, "Paw Paw is one smart man."

That night, after everyone was in bed, I penned a letter to Joe, who was now stationed in Pirmasens, West Germany. I did not write about my plight other than mention that Paw Paw was trying to put a little weight on us because he sent us a whole case of Mars Bars (Ha Ha).

Nineteen days later I received a letter from Joe. I unfolded the letter to reveal fifty dollars enclosed. Tears began to burn my eyes as I read the sweet words written on that paper. Joe ended his letter with:

"I hope you can use the money, Mom; after all,' it's a great life if you don't weaken, but who wants to be strong.'"

I smiled and hugged the letter to my chest. Alfred would have his class ring and just in time for his graduation.

I should have known better than to doubt God's ability because if He could turn water into wine, and feed five thousand with one boy's small lunch, He could certainly help me buy Alfred a graduation present.

CHAPTER EIGHTY-SEVEN

I made a trip to Dalymeyer's Jewelry Store the very next day and ordered Alfred's class ring. I so wanted Alfred to have that ring before he graduated. I met the mailman at the box every after- noon, as it was to be shipped straight to my home address. One week before graduation the anticipated package arrived.

My heart was racing as I took that box into the kitchen and removed the brown paper to reveal its contents. I picked up the heavy gold ring with its ruby red stone while reading the inscrip- tions: Jenkins Independent School- Class of 1959. For reasons unknown, the tears began to flow down my face like a river. I held tight to the ring in the palm of my hand as my mind drifted back to earlier times.

Alfred was my middle boy, and I knew often times he felt slight- ed due to his position in the family. Bonnie had always had the middle child syndrome and complained about always being over- looked. Although Alfred had never openly complained about it, Joe being my first, got all the attention for his first two years, and Norman, with his mischievous streak, required my constant focus and attention. All in all, Alfred had managed to fly under the radar.

I placed the ring back in the box and pulled a piece of paper and a pen from the kitchen counter and began writing:

My Dearest Alfred,

I just can't believe how fast you grew up and by this time next week will be a high school graduate. I am so proud of you and of the man you are becoming. I can close my eyes and still see that little boy, with his lip puckered and quivering, as I sent you to get your switch, and the sweet little boy with those sparkling blue eyes dancing as he rode his stick horse all around the yard.

I know from listening to Bonnie that being the one in the middle can be tough. If you ever felt less loved, just know that I wanted you before you were ever conceived, and I love every one of you kids just the same.

I never told you this Alfred, but you remind me so much of Will. You have his gentle spirit and kind heart which you both got from my momma. As long as you are in this world a piece of them will live also.

I want more than anything for you to achieve all your dreams and live happily ever after. You can accomplish this if you keep God close. Just know that He is only one breath away, and He is always ready to help when asked. In fact, He helped me get you this class ring.

I guess what I am trying to say in all this jumbled up mess is I love you with all my heart, and I am so proud and honored to be your momma.

I love you, Sugar,
Mom

I folded the letter and placed it alongside the ring in my apron pocket. When Alfred arrived home, I called him into the kitchen.

I looked up at him now some ten inches taller than myself. I handed him the letter and the ring. He bent down and kissed my forehead before heading off to his room.

He reemerged back in the kitchen a few minutes later with his class ring adorning his finger. He hugged me tight and whispered, "You're amazing, Mom. Thanks so much for my ring."

I whispered back, "Don't thank me; thank God."

CHAPTER EIGHTY-EIGHT

Following Alfred's graduation, Sue, Norman, Alfred, and I headed to Wilkesboro, North Carolina for the summer. There was a multitude of reasons for my decision to spend the summer of 1959 down in North Carolina.

First and foremost, I desperately needed a summer job since my hours at the school had been drastically cut. Secondly, I wanted to give my relationship with Jim some space, so I could find out if absence did indeed make my heart grow fonder. Thirdly, I wanted to put some distance between Alfred and Irene and get Alfred away from the temptation of working in the mines. Finally, the big Elmore reunion was being held at Yadkin Valley Baptist Church, just outside of Wilkesboro, the fourth Sunday in June, and I sorely wanted to attend, as I had not seen so many of my relative's in years.

All four of us crawled into the Nash Rambler that third week of June for our first trip back to Wilkesboro in ever so long. We all piled in on Bessie for the first few days, and during that time Alfred secured a summer job at Lowe's Supermarket as a bag boy.

I, too, looked for work, but my efforts were proving futile. That Sunday, at the Elmore family reunion, my cousin, Luster Elmore, informed me of summer job openings at Kings Knitting in Lenoir. Since he worked for Kings Knitting, he felt sure he could secure me one of the temporary summer positions.

The following week I moved in with Luster and Sylvia Elmore for the summer and began work at Kings Knitting. I left Sue and Alfred with Bessie for the summer, as Alfred was now working in Wilkesboro, and Sue wanted to spend time with her cousin, Grace.

I took Norman with me because I knew three would be too much for Bessie, and I really could not trust Norman to behave himself for the remainder of the summer without parental supervision.

By summer's end, I could hardly wait to get back to Jenkins. I missed Jim something fierce and Jim, too, was ready for my return. Alfred was also feeling the love pangs that distance can cause, as he had spent most of his summer earnings on stamps, having written to Irene almost every day.

While driving back home Alfred chimed in, "I can't wait to see Irene. I sure hope she is waiting on me. You know, Mom, if I can't have her, I don't want anyone else."

I could relate with his words because I felt the exact same way about Jim. I glanced over at Alfred, "You know something, time and distance is a true test of love, and it sounds to me like you are passing the love test with flying colors."

Alfred smiled, "I loved Irene the first time we met."

Norman replied, "Well, that's nothing, Alfred, I have fallen in love with hundreds of girls the first time I met them."

Sue then stuck out her tongue before adding her two cents, "Yuck, I never plan on loving any old, yucky boys."

I chuckled, "Well, there is one thing I have learned about love; it sure comes around when you least expect it."

As the kids continued to debate love, and all its pros and cons, I began thinking of Jim. All at once, I felt an urgency to get back to him. I pressed my foot against the gas pedal with ever increasing pressure as Cupid shot love arrows straight at my heart.

CHAPTER EIGHTY-NINE

We arrived back in Jenkins just as the sun began to fade from sight behind the Appalachian Mountains. I pulled the Nash Rambler into the driveway and hollered at my three kids, as they were all curled up sound asleep. We all grabbed a suitcase and headed toward the house. I could hear my phone ringing as I stuck the key into the lock on the back door. I knew it was someone calling our phone on the party line, as the ring was one long and two shorts. I threw down my suitcase, tripping over the footstool that set in front of the table that housed the phone. I banged into the table, reaching for the phone receiver. I instinctively knew that on the other end of that phone line was one of two people that I was eager to hear from, Jim or Joe. I picked up the receiver and placed it to my ear while catching my breath, "Hello."

On the other end I heard Jim's voice, "Well, Lucy you made it home. I sure have missed you."

My heart sped into overdrive and I blurted out, "Oh, Jim, I so missed you. It seems like forever since I saw you, and I really need to see you. When can I see you?"

My ears could not believe what they heard coming out of my mouth, but I couldn't seem to stop myself.

I heard Jim chuckle, "I would be happy to pay you a visit later this evening, but I know you must be tired?"

"I am never too tired to see you; in fact, the sooner the better."

What on earth was wrong with me? I needed to get hold of myself before I blurted out something on this party line that I would live to regret.

"Lucy, if you feel up to it, I will see you around eight."

"Perfect."

I hung up the phone and turned around. While rubbing her tired eyes, Sue looked up at me with an inquisitive look on her face, "Are we going to court Jim tonight?"

"No, but he is coming over, so I need you to help me get the suitcases upstairs before he gets here."

By the time Jim arrived, we had managed to get everything unpacked and ourselves freshened.

When I opened the door and saw him standing there, I reached out and hugged him tight. He leaned down touching his cheek to mine and whispered into my ear, "I love you, Lucy Hornaday." I closed my eyes and began swaying back and forth, while our cheeks remained firmly pressed together, just relishing the moment. Without any doubt, I knew my destiny for the second time in my life, and with my children's blessing I would not remain a widow for long.

CHAPTER NINETY

I thought once my kids reached adulthood all my worries would be over, but I was quickly finding out that is when the real worry begins. I had worried so long about Alfred and Irene prematurely tying the knot that I had not given thought to far worse things happening.

I could not believe my ears when Alfred announced over supper one evening in late August that he had joined the Marine Corp and would be leaving for Camp Lejeune in late September. I remember dropping my spoon, and the vegetable soup splattering my clothes and my freshly washed table cloth, as those words seemed to numb my whole body. Those stunning words left me immobile and speechless for several minutes. When I was able to release the words from my throat I said, "I knew in my heart you would be leaving soon, but I thought with a gold band on your finger not gold badges on your lapel."

I looked directly at Alfred, who now all but had his head down in his soup bowl. He never made eye contact, but talked to his soup as he began to explain, "I didn't mean to do it, Mom. Ralph and I went to Norton just to get information on the Marines. The recruiter kept talking about how great it was to be among the few, the proud, the Marines. He had us all charged up. Before we knew what was happening, we had signed a whole bunch of papers and were being seated for the ASVAB test. When I sat down to take the test, I started thinking about Irene. I knew I did not want to be so far away from her again, so I decided to purposely fail it. There is no way I passed that test! I could not have passed, but that officer made me a new recruit anyway. Before I could say anything, he gave me my papers to report for duty September 25th."

I processed Alfred's words in my mind before responding, "Thank you, Alfred."

He raised his head, his face holding a bewildered look, "What for?"

"For giving me advance notice. I don't think my heart could handle another one of my boys slipping off without as much as a goodbye."

A tear slid down Alfred's cheek, "I'm sorry I did it."

I tenderly smiled at Alfred, "Time flies, Sugar, and this, too, will pass."

Alfred departed from the Jenkins bus depot on September 25th, with Irene clinging to his arm, until the driver gave the last call for ticket holders.

Norman, Sue, and I watched as Alfred boarded and took a seat near the back. He opened his window and waved to us, as the bus made its way toward the highway.

I blew him a kiss and I watched as he caught it and put it in his shirt pocket. We all stood watching until the bus disappeared down the road.

We somberly got into our little Rambler and drove home. When I pulled into the driveway, Norman and Sue hopped out, but I lingered inside the car. I took in a long deep breath and stared at Norman and Sue sitting on the back stoop, as I ever so slowly exhaled. I opened the door, and while gazing at the controls along the Rambler's dashboard, I patted the steering wheel and said, "Things are forever changing around here, and I know you, old girl, are going to miss him as much as I will."

CHAPTER NINETY-ONE

With two of my boys now in the service our home seemed all but empty. I knew Norman was having an extra-hard time, with first Joe, and now Alfred being gone. The three of them had always shared a room and slept in the same bed, with Norman always in the middle, until Joe left last year. He now had the room and that big bed all to himself. That night after Alfred's departure, I decided to forego my date with Jim and spend the evening with Norman and Sue. I made homemade fudge, and we spent the evening listening to the radio and talking about old times. We sat up until almost midnight before finally making our way to bed.

Sue and I had just gotten settled in when Norman appeared in the doorway. "I don't think I am going to be able to sleep in that big bed all by myself."

I replied, "You can sleep with Sue and me."

He protested, "I'm not going to sleep with my momma and sister."

I laughed, "Well, suit yourself."

Norman turned and walked back to his room, only to return a short time later. He leaned down and whispered, "Ok, which side you want me to get in on?"

I slid to the middle of the bed patting the newly vacated spot. When we finally got settled in, Sue whispered, "Mom, tell us a happy story."

I began my story and in a few short minutes Norman and Sue were both sound asleep.

I thought back to my childhood when Bonnie, Bessie, and I shared a room and bed after Daddy married Bertha. I remembered the sense of security I felt when all of us snuggled down for the night. I rose up and peered at Norman on my left and Sue on my right. I gently kissed each one on the forehead and lay back on my pillow. I closed my eyes and prayed for God's hand of protection on Joe and Alfred and His continued mercy on us all.

Even though two of my babies had left my nest, I, again, felt that sense of security and a feeling of complete contentment as I snuggled down for the night with my babies that remained. I thought, I may have only two with me under this roof, but I still have all four with me under our great big sky.

CHAPTER NINETY-TWO

The older I got the more time seemed to speed up. Before I could even get fully turned around Christmas was peeking at me from behind the corner. With Joe and Alfred now away in service, and my cafeteria hours cut to nearly nothing, I knew I didn't have the money or the spirit to do Christmas justice. I made the decision to celebrate the season in a very practical way with Sue, Norman, and Jim.

With no extra money to purchase our Christmas tree, I decided that we would cut down our own. Eight days before Christmas we took a trip up into the woods to find our Christmas tree. It was not long before Sue fell in love with a scrawny, white pine. Actually, she fell in love with the bright red Cardinal that sat on the top branch of that lanky pine, and as she put it, "Sung its Christmas song for her."

I laughed out loud, "Sue, that tree is so scrawny and weak looking. I bet it won't hold more than four or five ornaments and only then if we brace the branches against the wall."

Sue then began to plead, "But, Momma, it needs a home for Christmas, too."

Norman did not even wait for a response. He just began sawing away on the trunk of that small sapling. By afternoon, we had our little tree up and decorated. Sue stood back after it was coated with mounds of silver tinsel and announced, "See, Mom, this is our good luck tree!"

While admiring the tree as its silver glistened, catching the last glimmers of sunlight peering through the window, I chuckled, "I hope it's lucky enough to start growing money!"

Norman interjected, "I hope it grows lots of presents in time for Christmas."

I felt my stomach wince because I knew that short of a miracle the presents would be scarce.

I did not sleep a wink that night. I tossed and turned, trying to figure out how I could create that Christmas magic for Norman and Sue with practically no money. I finally came to the decision that I would spend what little I did have on a Christmas feast; at least, the kids would have happy bellies. I made a trip to the Pine Store the following day and priced all the foods on my "wish list." I wrote each food down on my note pad, with its corresponding price next to the item. I, then, made my way home to begin finalizing my Christmas feast menu.

On my way back into the house, I stopped at the mailbox. On top of a stack of Christmas cards was a letter from Joe. I ripped open the envelope and began reading. About halfway down the page he wrote:

Mom, I got a 30 day pass, and I'm coming home for Christmas. I'll be in Bristol, Virginia on December 22nd, and I need someone to pick me up at the bus depot. If you can't make it, I will hitch a ride to Jenkins. Just know that I'm coming home.
I love you, Mom.
Joe

Oh my goodness, Joe was coming home! I ran through the door screaming, "Norman, Sue, Joe is coming home for Christmas!"

Sue looked at me before her eyes darted to our puny Christmas tree that stood in front of the window, "See, I told you it was our good luck tree."

I winked, "I sure hope you're right."

I immediately looked at my list and added confectioner's sugar and birthday candles; after all, my Christmas baby had to have a birthday cake.

The Monday before Joe's anticipated arrival, I scrounged together all the paper money and loose change I had, and I made another trip to the Pine Store, this time to purchase the groceries for our Christmas feast. I had enough money to purchase everything on my list and even had one dollar and thirty-four cents left over. I walked over to the candy counter and spent my last dollar on penny candy for the kids' stockings.

I drove home feeling good about my decision. When I pulled into the driveway, I noticed a foot locker under the mailbox. I stopped the car and walked over to take a look. The locker had been sent from Pirmasens, West Germany and under our address in big red letters were the words: **Place under the Christmas tree and don't open till Christmas!**

I hollered for Norman, and he peered from behind the door. "Norman, can you give me a hand with this trunk?"

Norman came running, "Where did that come from?"

I smiled, "Joe sent it, and I'm sure it's something for Christmas."

His eyes widened, "Do you think it's something for me?"

"I guess we will find out when Joe gets home."

Norman and I carried the trunk into the house and placed it under the tree.

While putting my groceries away, I heard Norman and Sue rustling about in the sitting room, and then I heard Sue squeal out as Norman shushed her. I dropped the sack of flour on the table and made my way to the sitting room to find Norman shutting the trunk lid. I opened my mouth to chasten him, but he looked at me with his mischievous eyes and said, "Don't say anything, Mom. I couldn't help myself. You won't believe how many presents are in this trunk. There is something for everyone! Sue was right; this is our lucky tree."

I could not help but get caught up in their excitement. I knew in my heart this Christmas would be perfect. I would be providing the feast, Joe would be providing the presents, and our little tree was proving to provide the luck we needed for a little Christmas magic.

CHAPTER NINETY-THREE

Norman, Sue and I picked Joe up in Bristol, Virginia on the afternoon of December 22nd and arrived back in Jenkins to a light dusting of snow. When Joe walked through the door and saw our Christmas tree, he burst out laughing. Sue gave Joe a puzzled look, "What are you laughing at?"

"That tree! Looks just like a space ship. I bet you'll find space aliens inside that trunk."

Sue smiled, "You can't fool me, Joe; I already know what's in the trunk because Norman showed me."

Joe frowned at Norman, "Can't you ever follow the rules? It says, "' **Don't open till Christmas**.'"

I decided to let Joe handle this situation and walked on into the kitchen to begin baking my Christmas cookies. I smiled as I listened to Sue and Norman telling Joe about that tree bringing them such good luck.

I spent the remainder of the afternoon making Christmas candy and cookies. The smell of baking cookie dough weighing heavy in the air, along with the soft snow falling outside the window, made it impossible not to catch the Christmas spirit. I began singing "Jingle Bells," and in a few short moments Sue, Norman, and Joe joined me in the kitchen. The three of them sat around the table nibbling on cookies, hot from the oven, as we sang all the Christmas carols we could remember. I had to admit this Christmas was turning out pretty perfect and I, too, was willing to give our little tree some of the credit it deserved.

I spent the following day tidying up the house and fixing all those make ahead dishes for our Christmas feast. I got out my best china dishes that had been packed away for years and washed each piece, remembering the first time I spotted them at the company store. I so longed for a set of the beautiful white dishes, trimmed in green, with beautiful bouquets of daisies adorning the center. Alexander surprised me with my first place setting on our second Christmas together. Over the next two years, he would purchase additional place settings as we could afford, until I had service for ten. I had always used them on holidays and for special meals until Alexander died, and sadly, I could not remember a single time I had used them since.

As I stood at the kitchen sink washing all that china, while watching the snow gather on the tree branches, memories of Christmases past flooded my mind. Before Alexander's death, Christmas had always been a time of great joy; after all, I had celebrated three of those Christmases with brand new babies. I so wanted to recapture all that joy I had felt in years past.

As I finished setting the table with my beautiful china, I felt the urge to set an extra place setting for Alfred. I knew it was crazy, but it was Christmas and maybe Santa could pick him up at Camp Lejeune and have him sitting under our little "space ship", as Joe called it, just in time for Christmas. I laughed out loud at my silly thought, but as I passed by our glistening tinseled tree on my way to bed, I felt a sort of magic in the air that you only feel when everything is coming together perfectly.

CHAPTER NINETY-FOUR

I awoke Christmas Eve to the voices of Joe, Norman, and ALFRED outside my bedroom door. I hurriedly got on my robe and ran to the door, flinging it open. There stood my Alfred in his Marine uniform looking taller and more handsome than I remembered. I flung my arms around his neck and said, "I know this is a dream, but I'm taking you with me when I wake up."

Alfred laughed, "It's not a dream, Mom. I just finished basic training, and I got a two week pass. I wanted to surprise you and Irene."

I squealed, "It's the best surprise ever! Having you and Joe back home, well, having all my babies here with me for Christmas is the best present in the whole wide world!"

I felt like I was walking on air the entire day.

That evening I invited Jim and Irene over for our traditional Christmas Eve meal consisting of food chopper sandwiches, home fries, and Christmas cookies. After supper, we all gathered around our little Christmas tree while Sue read the Christmas story from the second chapter of Luke.

As Sue read the story of that first Christmas, I affectionately glanced over at Joe, my Christmas baby. I thought back to that Christmas twenty years ago when I brought him into the world and how I exclaimed to Alexander and Dr. Higgins that he was the best Christmas present I had ever received!

I was startled from my daydream when Norman nudged me while asking, "Momma, can we open presents now?"

Joe jumped up from the couch and said, "Yes, we can!"

He made a bee-line for his trunk and opened it revealing wrapped presents for everyone, including Jim and Irene, along with at least two dozen 45's that we could listen to on our record player.

He handed me a wrapped box and I opened it; inside was a beautiful red sweater. Tears welled in the corner of my eyes. I hugged Joe while whispering, "Thank you so much, Sugar. I sure do love you."

Joe pulled back holding me at arm's length while saying, "'*It's a great life if you don't weaken.*'"

I joined in, "'*But who wants to be strong.*'"

After everyone had opened their presents, we put a stack of 45's on the record player, moved back the coffee table, and made room for a dance floor. We sang the lyrics to the songs we knew and danced to the ones we didn't. I could not remember ever having had more fun.

That night after Jim and Irene went home and all the kids were in bed, I filled stockings with oranges, nuts, and penny candy for each one and hung them from the bed posts. I then nestled in my bed beside Sue and took out my Bible. I opened it to my favorite Psalm that still housed my clover. I lifted the clover from the page and thanked God for keeping my kids safe and bringing us all together to celebrate His Son's glorious birth.

I awoke Christmas morning to Sue singing, "We Wish You a Merry Christmas," while chomping on a mouthful of bubble gum.

I walked across the hall to find that the boys were already up and gone. I made my way to the kitchen and found a note saying they had gone to pick up Irene and would be back soon.

I made me a cup of coffee and asked Sue what she wanted for breakfast. With bulging jaws she replied, "I already ate. I had an orange, some nuts, and a whole lot of candy."

Then I watched as she blew a bubble that seemed to consume her entire face. She soon disappeared into the sitting room and in no time I heard "The Duke of Earl" blasting from the record player speakers.

By noon, everyone was seated around the table for our Christmas feast, served on my best china dishes. I had made everyone's favorite food including my own comfort food- cornbread cakes. Jim patted me on the back and said, "Lucy, that meal would put Bogg's Lunch Counter to shame."

I humbly and graciously accepted his compliment, but inside I felt really proud because my Christmas feast was even better than I anticipated.

At four o'clock, we all gathered in the kitchen again to celebrate Joe's birthday. We were eating birthday cake and my homemade ice cream when Sue blurted out, "Look outside, it's snowing!"

I looked out the window as snowflakes the size of quarters splattered against the glass.

All the kids were soon outside playing in the snow, leaving Jim and me alone in the kitchen. I began cleaning up the dishes, and Jim walked into the sitting room. In no time, I heard the voice of Elvis singing, "Love me Tender."

As I turned to walk into the sitting room, there stood Jim in the doorway holding out his hand, "May I have this dance?"

I fell into his arms, and we danced in front of the window while I watched my kids out enjoying the snow.

I gazed down at our little Christmas tree, with its tinseled branches hanging ever closer to the ground. I winked at the tree and mouthed, "Thank you."

It seemed that the little tree stood a little taller and glistened even brighter. I was now convinced that tree had brought us luck because Christmas of 1959 turned out to be picture perfect.

CHAPTER NINETY-FIVE

Alfred did it. Against my better judgement, he really did it! Three days after Christmas he put that gold band on Irene's finger. What was he thinking? He was barely eighteen and Irene was but a child in my eyes. I knew better than to voice all my concerns, so I did the only thing I knew to do, I prayed that God would bless their union.

I knew I could not keep my babies under my wing forever, and even though it pained me, knowing they had grown up ever so fast, I did want them to venture out and find their happiness, too. Since both my boys would be returning to active duty soon, and Alfred now a married man I decided to fix the traditional New Year's Day meal and have all my kids, my new daughter-in-law, and Jim join me for supper. After all, we all needed all the good luck we could get leading into this brand new decade.

I spent my entire afternoon in front of the stove cooking black eyed peas, cabbage, hog jowl, cornbread cakes, Brown Pear Betty, and my homemade chocolate candy. As I stirred those simmering pots, I reflected over the last decade. The 1950's had brought

Kids and Cornbread Cakes

about heartache and celebration. I had lost the love of my life, but I had also found new love. With the Lord's help, I had raised two of my children to adulthood healthy and strong. I wondered what the 1960's had in store for me. I knew this decade ahead held more drastic changes, and I had to brace myself for a fast, bumpy ride.

I must have been completely caught up in my daydream because I did not hear Jim come into the house, walk up behind me, and wrap his arms around my waist. Completely startled, I hollered, "Whoop!" as I slung the hot chocolate candy that dripped from the spoon I was holding onto my hair and Jim's face.

Jim quickly grabbed the spoon from my hand, licking the remaining candy before it dripped onto the floor. I reached for a towel and wiped the chocolate from Jim's face before softly kissing his cheek. Jim smiled, "Can I help you with anything, Lucy?"

"Yes, you can gather everyone and get washed up because supper's almost ready."

In no time, everyone was sitting around the table, and for the second time in only a week, having a meal on my best china dishes.

I noticed that Alfred had a maturity about him that I had never noticed before. The shiny gold band on his finger proved he was a man, and it brought to mind Genesis 2:24: *For this reason a man shall leave his father and his mother and cleave to his wife and they shall become one flesh.* My stomach winced. Alfred was no longer mine but now Irene's.

I found myself getting all melancholy when Norman announced, "Mom, I'm getting married next! I have already narrowed it down to four girls, and which ever one accepts my proposal will be the future Mrs. Norman Hornaday."

I looked at Norman and said, "Now, you hold your horse's young man. You still have two years of school left and a whole lot of growing up to do. It's never a good idea to put the cart before the horse."

257

Joe eyed Norman, "If you have that many girls interested in you, heck, don't tie yourself down to one. Enjoy playing the field."

Alfred chimed in, agreeing with Joe.

Irene glared at Alfred, "You're not interested in taking your own advice, are you?"

Alfred took Irene's hand and said, "Honey, you're the only woman I see," before kissing her cheek.

Sue interjected, "Yuck, Alfred, don't do that at the table; it makes me sick."

After everyone was finished eating, we all remained around the table for the better part an hour discussing life and all its limitless possibilities.

Sue soon became bored with all the heavy talk and asked, "Who wants to play some records and dance?"

All the kids were soon dancing around the sitting room, as the record player blared, leaving Jim and me alone at the table.

Jim lovingly looked into my eyes and cupped his hand over mine that rested on the table. "Lucy, I hope I get to spend the rest of my life with you because you are truly the only woman I see."

I smiled, "I think I would like that, too, Jim Mann."

In this moment, I knew with a certainty that this decade would find me married once more.

CHAPTER NINETY-SIX

As Jim and I walked out of Preacher Byers house that Saturday afternoon, Sue ran and flung her arms around my neck and squealed, "We did it Mom! We finally married Jim."

I responded, "I reckon we did, Sue."

Sue had been out on every date with me for the past three years. Jim never seemed to mind our little "third wheel," but I knew he might protest her accompanying us for our honeymoon. I also knew better than to tell Sue that Jim and I were going on our honeymoon without her.

I had called Bessie the week before and asked if Sue could stay at her house for a few days and spend some time with her cousin, Grace. Bessie said she would love for Sue to stay. I had packed her a suitcase and put it in the back of Jim's Plymouth Station wagon without her knowledge. I knew I had to keep our honeymoon a secret from Sue, or she would be hounding us to go, too.

As soon as we pulled into Bessie's drive, Sue jumped out of the car and ran upon the carport to greet Grace. I heard her tell Grace, "Guess what? We married Jim!"

I watched as she and Grace disappeared into the house.

Bessie walked up behind the car as I was pulling Sue's suitcase from the back, "Well, Sis, I'm happy for you. Everyone needs somebody, and I couldn't have picked one any better for you."

I thanked Bessie and hugged her tight, before handing her Sue's suitcase. I scurried to get back into the car and out of the driveway before Sue noticed that we were leaving her behind.

As we headed down the road, Jim said, "This is the first time I've had you to myself, Lucy."

"I know, and it seems a little lonesome without some commotion coming from the back seat."

Jim smiled, "You're not missing her already....Are you?"

I looked down at my feet, "Well, maybe a little, but not enough to go back and get her."

Jim wiped his forehead, "Whew!" and leaned over and kissed my cheek.

When we returned, the following Monday afternoon, Sue met me at Bessie's door, with a furrowed brow and crossed arms.

I wrinkled up my nose, "Aren't you happy to see me?"

Sue pursed her lips, "Well, I wanted to go on a honeymoon, too. You know that I have never been on one before, and I can't believe you left without me."

I pulled Sue into my chest, "You will get to go on one someday, and I will let you go without me. How about that?"

Sue did not crack a smile. She got into the back seat, keeping her pouty face and sulking, for the entire ride back to Jenkins, Kentucky.

That evening, as I began unpacking our suitcases, I noticed a small notebook on top of Sue's packed clothes. I opened it to reveal these words in Sue's writing:

"April 7, 1962- Today we married Jim! I am happy. Mom's happy. I think the whole, wide world is happy!"

Sue walked in just as I was placing the notebook on the nightstand. Her smiling face signaled that she was over her mad spell. She put her arms around my waist and with fourteen year old maturity she said, "I'm glad we married Jim. He's a great addition to our family."

I nodded in agreement. For the first time since Alexander's death I felt that sense of security only a husband can bring.

CHAPTER NINETY-SEVEN

I did not realize what an eventful year 1962 would prove to be when I entered marital bliss. Within a week of our marriage, I found out that Alfred and Irene were expecting their first child. I could not believe that I was going to soon be a grandma. I went to the bedroom and picked up my Bible from the nightstand and opened it to Psalm 127. I peered down at my special clover. It seemed only a few days since I wished my babies on the clover, and now my babies were having babies. I could just hear Alexander saying, "We're about to be grandparents, Lucy, now what about that!"

In August of the same year, Joe surprised us all when he married Olsa Young. He and Olsa attended school together, but I never knew him to have a romantic interest in her, at least not before he left for the Army. Now that he and Alfred were both married, and, knowing how Norman looked up to his older brothers, I could only hold my breath and hope that he was not next.

That fall Norman did follow in his brothers footsteps, not by marrying, but by enlisting in the armed services. I did have some concerns because Norman was not as mature as his older brothers had been when they enlisted, but I had heard the Army could make a man out of a boy. I hoped they would make a man out of him, instead of killing him first.

Just as I did with Joe and Alfred, I wrote to Norman once a week, but unlike his brothers he never wrote back. After several weeks of my correspondence going unanswered, I began to worry. Maybe something bad had happened to my baby. After talking to Jim about my concerns, he encouraged me to put my worry to rest by calling and checking on him. I went straight to the phone and made a round of calls that led me to Norman's commanding officer. He picked up the phone and in a deep, gruff voice said, "Corporal Smith speaking."

His intimidating voice made me lose my words. I stammered around, "Ummm, Yes…..This is Lucy Hornaday….. Ummmm, I mean Lucy Mann. Well, anyway, I am Norman Hornaday's mother. Ummm……You do know Norman; don't you?"

He replied, "Yes ma'am. He is in my unit."

I, again, cleared my throat, "Wha… What I called for is to find out if he is ok?"

"He's fine ma'am. Why do you ask?"

"Well, I have been writing him for weeks, and I have not heard back a single word from him."

"I'll take care of it, and don't worry; you will hear from him real soon. Good day, Ma'am."

I felt relieved. "Thanks officer."

Ten days later I had my first letter from Norman, and it began with:

"Mom, why did you have to call my commanding officer?"

I laughed out loud when I read those words. Jim's advice worked because I never sent him another letter that went unanswered.

In October of the same year, I became the proud grandmother of a beautiful baby boy that Alfred and Irene named Alfred Jr. I could hear the pride and joy in Alfred's voice, on the other end of that phone line, as he announced, "Mom, I've got myself a boy, and he looks just like me."

My baby was now a proud Papa and I was officially a grandma. I had taken Jim's surname and the title of grandma all in the same year. This decade was just getting started, and with so many changes already, I felt that I might be in for the rollercoaster ride of my life.

CHAPTER NINETY-EIGHT

The following year, I began getting an itch to return to Wilkesboro, North Carolina. All my extended family was living in Wilkesboro, with the exception of Bonnie, who was still living in Dunham. With Joe and Alfred now married, Norman in the Army, and Sue only one year from graduation it seemed the perfect time.

Jim and I had a family meeting and discussed our plans with Sue. Sue was resistant as she wanted to graduate with her high school class in Jenkins, but Jim and I bribed her with a brand new piano and a telephone, and soon we were back in Wilkesboro. We moved to Roaring River and stayed with Joe and Olsa, while Jim looked for land to build our house.

In no time, Jim found the perfect piece of land in the Mount Pleasant Community and hired a contractor to build our home. We moved into an apartment in Wilkesboro where we lived while our house was under construction. I had no patience in waiting for our house to be built and worried Jim to death by continually asking, "How much longer?"

Jim said I was like a pesky kid in a car asking over and over "Are we there, yet?"

Jim knew that I liked things done quickly, but the building of our house was painstakingly slow.

To say that I was excited to move in eighteen months after we began construction, was an understatement. This two bedroom/one bath brick home with a full basement was my dream. The large eat-in kitchen with the beautiful built in cabinetry and ample counter space made me feel like I had died and gone to heaven. In all my years of living, I never imagined that I would have a home this nice, not to mention the ample yard space, with a perfect garden spot.

The night we moved in I made pinto beans and crisp cornbread cakes on my new stove. When Jim, Sue, and I sat down at the table, I said grace over the food and thanked God for His continued hand of mercy and unlimited blessings on me and my family.

After all three of us in unison said, "Amen" I looked over at Jim and said, "You know, God sure blessed me with good husbands. Alexander gave me my kids and, you, Jim, gave me my mansion."

Jim grinned, "Lucy, this little house is a far stretch from a mansion."

I responded, "Well, it sure is a mansion to me."

CHAPTER NINETY-NINE

We had not lived in our new house six months until Bonnie decided that she just had to move back to Wilkesboro, too. I knew she would eventually end up back here. Since I had been back, she had called at least once a week, moaning and groaning about her whole family up and moving one by one, and leaving her behind. I sensed her misery because I could hear it in her voice every time she called. I knew from my teenage years how heartsick it can make you having your whole family live at least one state away. I had an idea of how to get Bonnie back to Wilkesboro, but I needed to run it by Jim first.

The property that adjoined ours was up for sale, so I talked to Jim about the possibility of having Nathaniel and Bonnie as neighbors. Jim was up for whatever made me happy, and in no time, Nathaniel and Bonnie were back in Wilkesboro building their house "right on top of my tail," as I would jokingly say.

It felt good having my sisters and Daddy living close by, but neighboring with my sister did prove a little too close for comfort.

Bonnie was constantly meddling in my business and accusing me of meddling in hers. I knew we made better sisters than neighbors.

Bonnie openly admitted to enjoying a good fuss, and she knew the one thing that made my blood boil was her disputing our property boundaries. When she was in an arguing mood she would have me, as she put it, "walk the line" with her.

I remember one such argument that took place, in early fall, just after Sue entered college at Western Carolina. I was just beginning to adjust to my empty nest when Bonnie came down with a fresh batch of piping, hot yeast rolls. I got out some butter from the refrigerator, and we sat down at the table and began feasting on those light, airy rolls. I guess I must have been bellyaching a little about missing Sue, and not to be outdone, Bonnie started in on her hateful and demanding mother-in-law's upcoming week-long visit. I knew Bonnie well, and all this pent up stress made her want to fuss, so of course she brought up the property line. I really knew better than to let her get me so worked up, but I couldn't help myself. Soon Bonnie had me under her spell, and I was once again "walking the line."

Jim pulled into the driveway just as Bonnie blurted out, "That is not your bush, Lucy; it's mine. If I need to, I will prove it!"

I yelled back, "Well, you water it then! If it wasn't for the water out of my well, it would be dead."

Bonnie turned and stomped back up the hill toward her house and always having to get in the last word said, "Well, it says in the Good Book: "Thou shalt not cross thy neighbor's line."

I let out a long sigh.

Jim crawled out of the Plymouth with his pipe clinched between his teeth. He grinned, while his teeth held the pipe in place, and mumbled, "You, two, look like old sore-tailed cats. You know that not one handful of that dirt is going with you when you leave this world. If you keep getting your blood pressure up over this nonsense, you just might leave here quicker than you intended."

After I calmed down, I called Bonnie and apologized.

Bonnie had never been capable of saying I'm sorry, even as a child. I could remember as children, Momma, trying to get her to say I'm sorry for something she had done to Will, Bessie, or me. Bonnie would hold her breath and turn blue until she passed out. When she would regain consciousness, we would be so happy that she had not died that she never had to utter those words.

This particular day the words she said back to me was as close to an apology as I ever got from her. "Sis, I know you're missing Sue, and I just wanted to get your mind off her for a little bit. I hope you're feeling better, now."

I responded, "No need to hold your breath, Bonnie. I accept your apology."

CHAPTER ONE HUNDRED

E ven though my children were all grown and out from under my wing, they were still a source of worry, especially Norman. I was hoping that the military would make a man out of Norman like it did Joe and Alfred, but I could tell little difference in Norman when he returned home. He was the same free spirit that marched to the beat of his own drum.

Norman had a mischievous curiosity about him; he was born with it. I worried that this new hippie movement, a segment of the upcoming generation that was rebelling against society with its long hair, free love, and mood altering drugs would just suck him in.

I remember telling Jim, one evening, after spending hours trying to track Norman down, "I sure hope Norman gets married soon and settles down."

Jim looked from behind the paper he was holding in front of his face, "Lucy, help me figure this out. You didn't want Alfred and Joe to marry when they were ready to settle down, but you do want Norman to marry, and he's nowhere near settling down."

I sighed, "I'm hoping that marriage will make a man out of him because nothing else has worked."

Jim's eyes softened, "Norman is one of those that just has to learn things the hard way, and you need to stop rescuing him. Just let him be and learn his lessons on his own."

I felt tears pooling in the corners of my eyes, and I lowered my head before responding.

"Jim, you know I raised my four young'uns on a shoe string budget, with limited support from my family. I knew I could never amass a fortune to give them, but I always bought them the best foods I could afford, with the hope that if I fed them good nutritious food, they could grow up healthy and strong and go out and make their own fortunes. Joe, Alfred, and Sue all seem to be on the right track, and I am just trying to get Norman's wheels lined up on that track, too."

Jim leaned over his paper and kissed my forehead, "You need to quit worrying that sweet little head of yours, and let Norman be. Just give him some time and space, and give yourself some time and space."

By the time Norman finally married Janice Tugman on March 26, 1966, he had made an old woman out of me. It was no secret in my house that March was my bad luck month, and I had tried to get Norman to wait just a few more days for April to arrive. True to his nature he just smiled that mischievous smile and said, "Mom, I'm about to show you just how lucky March can be."

Norman was right in one respect because he gave me three beautiful granddaughters, all with March birthdays; however, that marriage was no match made in heaven. By late 1971, he was a free man again and like the song says "looking for love in all the wrong places."

CHAPTER ONE HUNDRED ONE

Sue decided to get married that same year that Norman divorced. She had dated Rainer Lowe all through college, and they seemed a perfect match. They married on April 10th in our new home, and true to my word, I let her go on her honeymoon without me.

I knew it would be a huge adjustment for me to have all my children out of the house. Even though Sue had been away at college, she did come home on weekends and holidays, where her room awaited her with all her things. Now the room was barren of Sue's belongings and only the furniture remained.

I walked into her empty room the morning after she married and sat down on the bed and began to cry. It's really hard to explain my emotional state. The tears were a mixture of sadness, joy, and relief. I was sad that my baby was gone, but I was also happy that she had found her mate and relieved that I had finally finished raising all four of my kids. I must have sat on Sue's bed for a better part of an hour daydreaming about old times when Jim peeked into the room. I smiled at Jim, and he came in and sat down beside me. He placed his hand on my knee and said, "How about a trip to the lake?"

I responded, "You mean to fish?"

His eyes lit up, "Yes! I think it will do you good to get out of this house and out on the water."

Jim had an old fishing boat that he loved taking out on the lake. He could spend the entire day inside a lake cove casting out his baited line in attempts to catch catfish and crappies. I did occasionally enjoy going along for the trip and would most times stretch out and listen to bullfrogs croak, birds sing, and insects buzz, while we bobbed up and down in the lake swells.

I kissed Jim's cheek, "Let's see if Bonnie and Nathaniel would like to join us."

In less than one hour, we had Jim's boat hooked to our Plymouth, and all four of us were headed for the lake. Once the boat was launched, Jim took off for his favorite cove, while the three of us sat back and enjoyed the ride.

Once inside the cove, Nathaniel and Jim baited all our hooks, and we sat back to fish. There was an unspoken rule when you fished with Jim and that was "Absolutely No Talking Allowed." This particular day, I was happy to follow his rule because I wanted some time to lean back, soak in the sun, and process these new thoughts and feelings I was experiencing.

We must have fished for over three hours with no one getting even as much as a nibble. I opened one eye and looked over at Jim, as he reeled in his wormless hook, while chewing on the cigar that hung from the corner of his mouth. Nathaniel stood up and bent over Bonnie to get the bait jar, and in the deafening silence of that cove, he farted. I opened my other eye and laughed out loud. Since Nathaniel had already broken the "code of silence" I said, "That's right Nathaniel, if you can't catch them, just shoot them."

Everyone began to chuckle and laugh, as Jim took the driver's seat and started the motor. Since the "fishless" stress seemed to be getting the better of Nathaniel, we decided to call it a day. Even though we did not catch or "shoot" a single fish, this day was just what the doctor ordered. I had this time out in nature to reflect over my life. I knew, even though all my children were on their own, I still had Jim with me, and his peaceful, easy presence brought me much contentment and joy.

CHAPTER ONE HUNDRED TWO

Thanksgiving of 1972 was to be a big event at my house. It was the first Thanksgiving, in ever so long, that I would have all my kids, spouses, and grandchildren under the same roof. I also invited Daddy and Bertha to join us for Thanksgiving dinner.

The Friday before Thanksgiving I went to the grocery store to purchase my turkey. I decided to get the biggest bird available, as I wanted everyone to leave my table "stuffed." I dug through all those frozen turkeys until I found the perfect thirty pound bird. It was all I could do to hoist it over into my grocery cart.

Once home, I had Jim carry the turkey into the house while I cleared off and removed the bottom rack in my refrigerator to make room for the great big gobbler. As Jim placed the turkey in the refrigerator, he said, "I didn't know you were inviting the entire county for Thanksgiving, but you must be because there is no way that just our family could ever eat this monster of a bird."

I wrinkled my nose and chuckled, "I want to make sure that no one leaves my table hungry."

I had to admit every time I opened the refrigerator and peered down at that turkey I got a little nervous. I knew cooking this massive bird would be a feat.

On Wednesday morning, I decided to go ahead and dress the bird and get it ready to roast. I lugged the turkey from the refrigerator, placed it in the sink, pulled the giblet bag from deep inside the chest cavity, and washed it thoroughly. I got out my roasting pan and began wrestling with the turkey, trying to fit it inside. I soon found that my turkey roaster was no match for this thirty pound bird.

I took out my butcher knife and cut off its legs and again tried to stuff it into the pan... didn't fit. I took that same knife and cut off its wings....still didn't fit. I wrestled around with that bird for half a day, and when it was all said and done, I had a very large turkey breast remaining in my roaster, with its remaining parts buried in the back yard behind my garden.

I spent the remainder of the evening and into the wee hours of the morning peeling, cooking, and baking in preparation for our noontime meal.

When I finally did get into bed, I again wrestled with that turkey in my sleep. I awoke on Thanksgiving morning completely exhausted. I walked into the bathroom, splashed my face with water, and combed my hair before entering the kitchen. Jim was sitting at the table reading the newspaper and drinking his morning coffee. He caught sight of me as I crept past him on my way to the oven to check the turkey. Noticing my red swollen eyes and my slow shuffle he said, "Looks like that turkey has about got the best of you."

I laughed out loud, "I reckon so."

By noon, our house was crammed with all my children, their spouses, Norman's new girlfriend, all the grandchildren, along with Daddy and Bertha. After the blessing, everyone filled their plate and found a place to sit down and enjoy our feast.

After eating, the kids retreated to the front yard to play a little football, and Jim and Daddy took their position in front of the television. I began clearing the kitchen with Bertha's help. I noticed that she kept rubbing her head and squinting her eyes. As I was putting the last of the clean dishes away, Bertha said, "I think your daddy and I will go ahead and leave because I have a terrible headache and need to go lie down."

I really did not think much of it because it seemed that something was always troubling Bertha. After she and Daddy left, I spent the rest of the evening in motherly bliss – enjoying my wonderful gifts from God.

After everyone left, I retreated to my bed completely exhausted. I don't think I even moved until the ringing of the telephone woke me midmorning. I staggered to the phone, and it was Daddy on the other end. He said that Bertha had been up all night with a terrible headache and he wanted to see if I could talk her into going to the doctor.

Daddy got Bertha on the line, but there was no talking Bertha into seeing the doctor. She was adamant that doctors were the only people who could kill you and get by with it, and she had no intentions of going to the doctor unless she got snake bit.

Daddy just decided to let Bertha be; however, on Sunday evening Daddy called me in a frantic state. He said that Bertha had passed out, and he had called the ambulance. He asked me to meet them at the hospital.

I had Jim drive me to Wilkes General Hospital where I met Daddy in the emergency room. He was a ball of nerves, wringing his hands, and saying over and over, "I should have insisted that she see the doctor."

I sat with Daddy the remainder of the evening, and into the night, awaiting the outcome of Bertha's tests. After midnight, the doctor finally appeared from behind the curtain with the news, "Bertha has a brain hemorrhage, and short of a miracle will never regain consciousness."

Daddy buried his face in his hands and began to sob. I put my arms around my daddy's shoulders and hugged him tight. Like we did with Momma, Daddy and I stayed by Bertha's side until she passed early Monday morning.

Daddy, too, brought Bertha back home for her wake. I grieved as I watched Daddy take hold of her hand as the tears poured from his eyes.

I thought back to my childhood and the stories told about how much my momma wanted me- how she trained me to help take care of my siblings and Daddy. With Bertha's passing, Daddy was once again my responsibility, and I would do my very best to take care of him to honor my momma's wishes.

CHAPTER ONE HUNDRED THREE

J ust when you think that nothing else can shock you, something happens that knocks you off your feet. I experienced the shock of my life in late August 1980. This was the day that I received a telephone call from Shady Pines Rest home. The nurse on the other end asked to speak to Lucy Elmore. It took me a second to realize that she was talking about me. I responded, "Speaking."

"Ms. Elmore, Albert Bell has been insisting for the last several days that I give you a call. He says he needs to see you. Are you family?"

I felt a shockwave shoot up my spine, "Well, he married my aunt if you call that family."

There was a moment of silence before she said, "He really wants to see you. Can I tell him that you will be visiting soon?"

I felt my arms and legs began to tremble, and I could feel a cold sweat break out on my forehead. I did not know what to say, but the silence was growing ever more awkward so I just blurted out, "Sure," and hung up the phone.

I sat on the couch for several minutes contemplating what Albert could want with me? I knew I needed to bite the bullet and go ahead and get this over with because putting it off would just be torturous.

I went into the bathroom and freshened myself, then to the closet and pulled out one of my light weight sweaters. Even though the afternoon was sweltering hot, I wanted to make sure that none of my skin was exposed when I went in to see Albert.

I walked out to the car and hollered for Jim, who was piddling down in the garden. I told him that I was going to the rest home, and I would be back shortly.

As I pulled into the parking lot of Shady Pines, my legs and arms began to tremble again. I pulled into a parking space and turned off the ignition as my whole body began seizing and shaking. I said out loud, "Lucy, you get a hold of yourself. You have no reason to be acting like this. He can't do anything to you now."

I bowed my head and said, *"Help me Dear Lord I pray,"* before taking in a deep breath and stepping out of the car.

Immediately upon entering the facility a pretty, blonde nurse's aide asked if she could help me.

I replied, "Yes, can you tell me Albert Bell's room number."

She smiled, "Room 412 ...by the way, are you Lucy Elmore?"

I smiled back, "Yes."

She said, "I'm glad you came. Do you want me to show you to his room?"

I replied, "Thanks, but I think I can find it."

As I walked down that long hall toward Albert's room my heart began to race, and I again began to shake. When I reached his door I took the sweater from my arm and put it over my shoulders.

I took a moment to calm myself before stepping inside the doorway. As soon as I saw Albert sitting in a wheel chair over in the far corner of the room, I was fourteen years old again as all those memories came flooding back.

I could tell the way his head and shoulders were slumped that he was dozing. I stood in that doorway for at least five minutes just staring at him, really not knowing what to say. I finally got up my nerve, cleared my throat, and said, "Albert, it's me, Lucy."

He slowly lifted his head and looked in my direction. He had a confused look on his face, and I again said, "Albert, it's me, Lucy Elmore. The nurse said you wanted to see me."

Albert lowered his head, cupping it in the palm of his hand. He shifted in his chair and began to speak, "Lucy, I am so glad you came. There is something I have wanted to tell you for a long time, and I just couldn't seem to get up the nerve to do it. Well, you know I'm not long for this world, Lucy, and I don't want to leave it with unfinished business. I need to tell you that I'm sorry for the wrong I did you and ask that you forgive me."

I felt a tear forming in the corner of my eye. I could not bring myself to move any closer toward Albert, but standing inside that doorway I looked him straight in the eye and said, "Uncle Albert, I forgive you."

I had never realized how much the abuse and not being heard or believed when I disclosed it had weighted me down, but I left Shady Pines that day a free woman. What I had endured as a teenager was finally admitted to and validated.

Jim was sitting at the kitchen table when I walked through the door. He said, "Lucy, you sure have a spring in your step."

I smiled, "I reckon I do because I was just released from my chains and fetters."

Jim looked bewildered.

I sat down beside Jim and I told him, for the first time, my story of the time I spent with Aunt Pandy and Albert. After I finished, I smiled and said, "Today Uncle Albert asked for my forgiveness, and I did the only thing I knew to do, I forgave him, and it really feels good."

CHAPTER ONE HUNDRED FOUR

When I married Jim I was well aware of our age difference, but I had not thought about how that might translate into me being left without a mate before I, too, entered into old age. I know it would have made no difference if I had entertained that thought because I loved and respected Jim, and I felt his love and respect in return.

Jim was a diabetic and had taken daily insulin shots ever since I had known him. He had, on a couple of occasions, gone into "sugar shock," scaring me so much that I insisted that he keep rock candy in his shirt pocket at all times.

Jim had lately been experiencing some dizzy spells that he attributed to his diabetes, but we were planning a big fishing trip to Augusta, Georgia the third weekend in March of 1981, and he intended to go. His cousins, Elmer and Edna, invited us to visit every few months, and Elmer loved to fish as much as Jim. Those two would spend the entire day out on the lake fishing. More times than not, they would return home with a cooler of crappies that were already cleaned and fileted.

Edna and I would fry those fish, along with homemade French fries and hushpuppies, and we would eat until we were "stuffed to the gills."

Due to Jim's dizzy spells, I made sure we had an ample supply of rock candy for the trip. The Thursday morning of our departure, Jim went out to hitch the boat to our Plymouth. I was back in the bedroom packing our suitcase when I heard Jim come back inside and groan as he sat down at the table. I knew he had not been outside long enough to hitch the boat, so I hollered from the bedroom, "Jim, are you ok?"

He did not respond.

I walked into the hallway and saw Jim slumped at the kitchen table. I ran over to him and pulled his head back. I shook his shoulders, but he did not respond. I ran to the phone and called for an ambulance.

Once we got Jim into the emergency room, I told the doctor that Jim had diabetes and had experienced incidents of "sugar shock." The doctor just seemed to disregard what I was suggesting and said that he would handle Jim's situation. He placed Jim in intensive care with strict visitation regulations, and I was unable to sit by his bedside.

For three days I begged the doctors that were attending to Jim to please check his insulin, but my requests fell on deaf ears. I remembered Bertha saying that doctors were the only ones who could kill you and get by with it, and I was beginning to think that she might have been right.

I spent those three days at the hospital praying for God to spare Jim's life. March had always been my bad luck month, and I could not stand the thoughts of losing Jim, especially not in March and so close to the time that I lost Momma and Will.

I had just gotten home the night of March 24th when I got that dreaded telephone call informing me that Jim had passed.

Sitting there alone I screamed out to God:

"Alexander died in the belly of that cold, coal mine without my hand to hold, and now Jim has died in that cold hospital the same way! Why did you have to take him in March, God? Why? Why? Why?!"

I rocked back and forth releasing all my pain and anguish through my moans and tears until nothing was left but those body jerking snubs.

I wiped my eyes and curled up in the corner of the couch as a warm, sweet peace seemed to envelope me.

God understood my heartache. He may have taken Jim in March, but that night He also took away my fear of being left alone. We may not always understand God's ways, but He will never burden us down with more than we are able to haul.

CHAPTER ONE HUNDRED FIVE

Following Bertha's death, I had taken on the responsibility of caring for Daddy. He had eaten practically every meal with me since she passed. Before Jim's passing, Daddy had been a constant fixture at our dinner table, and Jim never said a word.

Not long after Jim died, Daddy's health, too, began to decline. It was first one thing and then another. Just like Bertha, Daddy did not like doctors. Bonnie, Bessie, and I did talk him into seeing a doctor when he developed a huge knot on the side of his neck. The knot turned out to be cancer, and he agreed to some radiation treatments. That ordeal just made him hate doctors and hospitals all the more, and after his last radiation treatment he swore off doctors completely.

About a year after his cancer treatments, he began having issues with his kidneys. It was all downhill from there. Bonnie, Bessie, and I knew that Daddy's health was in a rapid state of decline, and we determined that leaving him alone would not be wise. We decided to take turns staying with Daddy, each of us spending every third day and night at his house. It was not long before his kidneys began to fail, and try as we might, we could not get him to see a doctor. As Daddy got sicker, I would pray that God would not take him on my watch. God did answer my prayer, as I was not present when he slipped out on October 5, 1984.

Losing Daddy was almost like losing Momma all over again. Even though I was sixty-four years old, I felt like that eleven year old girl. It sounds funny to say at my advanced age, but I was an orphan.

At Daddy's wake, I reached down and patted his hand and whispered, "Tell Momma I love her, and I'm still trying to keep my bright light shining."

A philosopher said it best when he said, *"With great love comes great loss."* Losing Daddy was my greatest loss ever because he was the last person in this world that loved me unconditionally. It truly is, *"a great life if you don't weaken, but who wants to be strong."*

CHAPTER ONE HUNDRED SIX

I t struck me funny as I climbed into the back of Norman's vehicle on May 26, 1996 that I was on my way to Sue's third wedding with Norman and his fourth wife. To think that I worried so much about Alfred getting married too young, yet his was the only marriage that had proved the test of time. Even my Joe did not get it right the first time, but he seemed to have found his perfect match the second time around.

The thought caused me to chuckle as I plopped down in the back seat. When my bottom hit the seat, I felt a pop in my back, as intense pain radiated up my entire spine. I gasped in pain, but I did not say a word. Today was Sue's special day, and I did not want to be a "Debbie Downer."

By the time we returned home, I had to have Norman's help to get out of the car. I assumed after a long, hot shower and a good night's rest I would be as good as new.

I awoke the following morning, and when I attempted to raise myself out of bed, I felt the most intense pain radiate down my back, taking my breath away. When I finally pulled myself out of bed, I put on my robe and went to the kitchen window. I spied Joe out doing his morning walk, as he lived just down the road from me. I hobbled to the front door and called for Joe.

As he made his way onto the porch he said, "What on earth happened to you, Mom, to stoop you over like that?"

I told him about my back popping the day before and how much pain I was experiencing. He said that I needed to see a doctor right away.

I was in so much pain that I didn't even protest. I looked up at Joe and said, "What doctor do I see? I haven't been to the doctor since Sue was a baby."

Joe called Norman since he was forever seeing a doctor for one thing or the other. Norman immediately got me an appointment to see his doctor in Blowing Rock.

Sue and Norman accompanied me to the doctor on that late spring day. Dr. Dunn immediately wanted x-rays of my back, which revealed numerous cracks in my spine. He decided on hormone therapy as a treatment, but said that I must first have a physical to make sure I was well enough for the treatment. I was seventy-six years old and had lived this long without a physical. I really could see no need in all that, now. I protested, but Sue and the doctor won out.

The doctor looked at me with concerned eyes as he did my breast exam. He fingered with the knot in my left breast and said, "How long has this been here?"

I replied, "Probably five years. It has never hurt or given me any problems, and I have just let it be."

He then got all scholarly and in a serious tone he said, "I don't think that was wise, Mrs. Mann, and I am going to send you for a mammogram."

Once I got my mammogram, it seemed that all attention focused on my breast that did not hurt, with no attention to my back that was killing me. I decided if I could get out of this ordeal unscathed, I would never complain to anyone, ever, again.

The following week, Sue took me to Greensboro to see a surgeon at Moses Cone Hospital. The doctors, nurses, and even Sue seemed to be so concerned with my breast. After several tests, the doctor came in and said, "Mrs. Mann, you have cancer, and we need to remove your breast as soon as possible."

I furrowed my brow and shrugged my shoulders as I spoke, "Why, I don't have breast cancer, and I don't know what all this fuss is about."

The short pudgy surgeon, whose name I can't remember, stood as erect as he could stand, sucked in his gut and said, "You do have breast cancer, and I need to remove it immediately."

I flailed my hand in the air, "Well, if you want it that bad, just take it!"

The following week that surgeon removed my left breast. I never believed that I had cancer, for some unknown reason, that doctor just took a liking to my breast and wanted it for himself.

As I was getting into the shower a few months after my surgery, I looked at my sunken chest through the mirror before rubbing my hand across the scar. A smile crept across my face as I spoke to my reflection, "This is not so bad. It was a win/win for me; after all, if it was cancer, it's gone, and even if it wasn't cancer, that doctor got what he wanted in the end. If he's happy with my breast, I can, most certainly, be happy living without it."

CHAPTER ONE HUNDRED SEVEN

I had learned through the years that the Lord will always give you exactly what you need, and He will also take away what He feels is necessary. With that said, the Lord chose to begin taking away my short term memory around 2003. As best as I remember, it was around the same time that Norman was diagnosed with cancer. I know the Lord did that to shelter me from all the agony that goes along with losing a child. I do remember Norman moving in with me shortly before he left this world. I did my best to take care of him, but neither I nor the doctors could save him.

I remember getting up the morning he passed. I didn't remember Sue, Alfred, and Joe coming to visit, but they must have because they were all here. I called for Norman, and Alfred met me in the kitchen. I think he told me that Norman had passed.

I remember my legs buckling under me, and Alfred catching my limp body before I fell to the floor. In a matter of minutes, I could not remember what happened to Norman.

Two days later, I remember going to a funeral, and I think it was Norman's, but then I can't remember if it really was his funeral or just that of a friend.

I think that I remember Sue staying with me the night we buried Norman.

When I went to bed that night, I took out my Bible and opened it to the Psalm that sheltered my four leaf clover. As I gently picked up that brittle clover, I noticed that one of its petals remained in the crease of my Bible. My four leaf clover had lost a petal. I felt a tear slip down my cheek and fall onto that lone petal that remained tucked inside that Psalm. It was then I realized the significance of that clover. I had wished for my babies on that clover when I was a mere child and just like that clover with its four petals, God had blessed me with four children. Now that Norman was gone, my clover, too, had lost a petal leaving behind only three. I breathed that Psalm again: "*Lo, children are an heritage of the Lord: and the fruit of the womb is his reward.*"

I gently placed my broken clover next to its fallen petal and closed my Bible holding it tight to my chest. I lay back in my bed and peered out the window into the starry heavens, and in a trembling voice I said, "*The Lord giveth and the Lord taketh away, blessed be the name of the Lord.*"

CHAPTER ONE HUNDRED EIGHT

I can't remember much about my last days. I was pleasantly confused much of the time, as cobwebs seemed to cover parts of my brain, clouding my memories and thoughts. I knew I wanted to be home, but I could not remember where home was for me anymore. I tried hard to remember day to day events, but the more I tried to remember the more I seemed to forget. As my final days drew to a close, I seemed to be more confused and much of the time I could not even find the words I wanted to say.

I do, however, vividly remember my dying process. I had always had a fear of the Great Unknown and always felt that I needed someone to go with me. Casper said in his movie that dying is like being born, only in reverse. Well, for me it was so much more than that. It was no longer something to fear but a wonderful experience to embrace.

As I lay in that bed so peacefully sleeping, I managed to somehow slip out of my body and visit my three living loving dolls that

I was leaving behind. I gently kissed each one on the cheek as they lay sleeping. I whispered to each of them, "I love you, and I'm going to check on Norman now. I'll be watching and waiting for you."

With a tear in my eye and a smile on my face, I took hold of the hand of Jesus. I felt as light as a feather as we ascended past the moon, planets, and all the millions of stars. I now knew where home is, and I was finally going home- and the best part – I will never again have to leave.

As significant or insignificant as you think my life has been, this is my story as I lived it, and despite all the pain and disappointments I endured, **<u>I truly loved my life</u>**.

EPILOGUE

Following Lucy's memorial service, as I am getting into my car to leave, I catch a glimpse of a large object in the sky. I watch as it flies closer, and I recognize it to be a beautiful Blue Heron. It flies directly over my head and on toward the huge fluffy wind clouds floating across the sky. It's as if I can feel Lucy's spirit on its wings as it disappears into the clouds.

I close my eyes for a moment, humming Lucy's song, while imagining her grand entrance into heaven. There she is walking through the gate with all her loved ones gathered round. I can envision the gleam in her eyes and the pure love on her face as she greets each of them with, "I love you, Sugar. You sure look pretty," before announcing, "Now, who would like a cornbread cake?"

Made in the USA
Columbia, SC
24 June 2023